THE STATES AND THE NATION SERIES, of which this volume is a part, is designed to assist the American people in a serious look at the ideals they have espoused and the experiences they have undergone in the history of the nation. The content of every volume represents the scholarship, experience, and opinions of its author. The costs of writing and editing were met mainly by grants from the National Endowment for the Humanities, a federal agency. The project was administered by the American Association for State and Local History, a nonprofit learned society, working with an Editorial Board of distinguished editors, authors, and historians, whose names are listed below.

Illinois

A Bicentennial History

Richard J. Jensen

W. W. Norton & Company, Inc.
New York

American Association for State and Local History
Nashville

Copyright © 1978
American Association for State and Local History
All rights reserved

Published and distributed by W.W. Norton & Company, Inc.
500 Fifth Avenue
New York, New York 10036

Library of Congress Cataloguing-in-Publication Data

Jensen, Richard J
  Illinois.

  (The States and the Nation series)
  Bibliography: p.
  Includes index.
  1. Illinois—History. I. Title. II. Series.
F541.J46   977.3′04   77–17626
ISBN 0-393-05596-5

Printed in the United States of America
1 2 3 4 5 6 7 8 9 0

For my mother

Contents

Illustrations

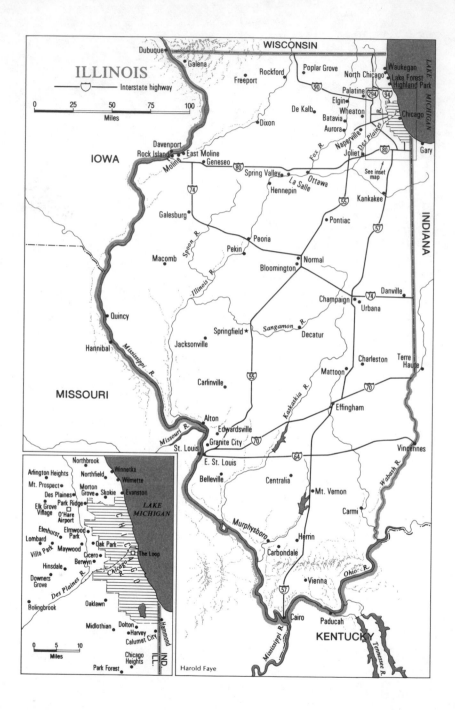

Invitation to the Reader

IN 1807, former President John Adams argued that a complete history of the American Revolution could not be written until the history of change in each state was known, because the principles of the Revolution were as various as the states that went through it. Two hundred years after the Declaration of Independence, the American nation has spread over a continent and beyond. The states have grown in number from thirteen to fifty. And democratic principles have been interpreted differently in every one of them.

We therefore invite you to consider that the history of your state may have more to do with the bicentennial review of the American Revolution than does the story of Bunker Hill or Valley Forge. The Revolution has continued as Americans extended liberty and democracy over a vast territory. John Adams was right: the states are part of that story, and the story is incomplete without an account of their diversity.

The Declaration of Independence stressed life, liberty, and the pursuit of happiness; accordingly, it shattered the notion of holding new territories in the subordinate status of colonies. The Northwest Ordinance of 1787 set forth a procedure for new states to enter the Union on an equal footing with the old. The Federal Constitution shortly confirmed this novel means of building a nation out of equal states. The step-by-step process through which territories have achieved self-government and national representation is among the most important of the Founding Fathers' legacies.

The method of state-making reconciled the ancient conflict between liberty and empire, resulting in what Thomas Jefferson called an empire for liberty. The system has worked and remains unaltered, despite enormous changes that have taken place in the nation. The country's extent and variety now surpass anything the patriots of '76 could likely have imagined. The United States has changed from an agrarian republic into a highly industrial and urban democracy, from a fledgling nation into a major world power. As Oliver Wendell Holmes remarked in 1920, the creators of the nation could not have seen completely how it and its constitution and its states would develop. Any meaningful review in the bicentennial era must consider what the country has become, as well as what it was.

The new nation of equal states took as its motto *E Pluribus Unum*—"out of many, one." But just as many peoples have become Americans without complete loss of ethnic and cultural identities, so have the states retained differences of character. Some have been superficial, expressed in stereotyped images— big, boastful Texas, "sophisticated" New York, "hillbilly" Arkansas. Other differences have been more real, sometimes instructively, sometimes amusingly; democracy has embraced Huey Long's Louisiana, bilingual New Mexico, unicameral Nebraska, and a Texas that once taxed fortunetellers and spawned politicians called "Woodpecker Republicans" and "Skunk Democrats." Some differences have been profound, as when South Carolina secessionists led other states out of the Union in opposition to abolitionists in Massachusetts and Ohio. The result was a bitter Civil War.

The Revolution's first shots may have sounded in Lexington and Concord; but fights over what democracy should mean and who should have independence have erupted from Pennsylvania's Gettysburg to the "Bleeding Kansas" of John Brown, from the Alamo in Texas to the Indian battles at Montana's Little Bighorn. Utah Mormons have known the strain of isolation; Hawaiians at Pearl Harbor, the terror of attack; Georgians during Sherman's march, the sadness of defeat and devastation. Each state's experience differs instructively; each adds understanding to the whole.

The purpose of this series of books is to make that kind of understanding accessible, in a way that will last in value far beyond the bicentennial fireworks. The series offers a volume on every state, plus the District of Columbia—fifty-one, in all. Each book contains, besides the text, a view of the state through eyes other than the author's—a "photographer's essay," in which a skilled photographer presents his own personal perceptions of the state's contemporary flavor.

We have asked authors not for comprehensive chronicles, nor for research monographs or new data for scholars. Bibliographies and footnotes are minimal. We have asked each author for a summing up—interpretive, sensitive, thoughtful, individual, even personal—of what seems significant about his or her state's history. What distinguishes it? What has mattered about it, to its own people and to the rest of the nation? What has it come to now?

To interpret the states in all their variety, we have sought a variety of backgrounds in authors themselves and have encouraged variety in the approaches they take. They have in common only these things: historical knowledge, writing skill, and strong personal feelings about a particular state. Each has wide latitude for the use of the short space. And if each succeeds, it will be by offering you, in your capacity as a *citizen* of a state *and* of a nation, stimulating insights to test against your own.

James Morton Smith
General Editor

Preface: Illinois as the Microcosm State

ILLINOIS, at the center of America's heartland, has for more than a century been a crossroads state. The nation's great transportation arteries—the Mississippi and Ohio rivers, the Great Lakes, the transcontinental railroads, the network of interstate highways, the routes of the airlines—all intersect in Illinois. Most Americans have probably travelled through the state, noticing the former prairie now devoted to corn and soybeans, stopping over in Chicago, perhaps even visiting the small towns or the Lincoln shrines. Tens of millions have lived in Illinois for shorter or longer periods, people from all parts of the nation and a hundred foreign countries. They came not to enjoy the hot, wet summers and blustery winters, but to earn a good living, for the prairie soil has been fertile, the factories and mines generally productive, the offices and stores usually busy, the entertainment districts endlessly lively. The blend of people of all races, religions, and nationalities, living on farms, in towns, cities, and suburbs has made Illinois a microcosm of the United States. The story of Illinois is the saga of the hopes, fears, aspirations, and achievements of its people; in ways I will try to identify, it is America's story too.

Almost everyone knows something of the history of Illinois from the lives of Abraham Lincoln, Jane Addams, Clarence Darrow, Al Capone, Richard Daley, and other heroes, heroines, or villains. Certain great events in the state's history are well-known also—the Black Hawk War, the Lincoln-Douglas debates, the Chicago Fire, the Haymarket Riot, the Pullman Strike, the Saint Valentine's Day Massacre, the atomic chain reaction under Stagg Field, the riots at the 1968 Democratic Convention. From great personalities and spectacular events, however, one does not learn much about the totality of life in a state. The chronicles of dates of lesser events and names of governors, generals, and other minor figures that characterize textbook history provide even less understanding. Illinois has been a microcosm of America because its history exhibits basic conflicts that had much to do with shaping American society in general. Riots, strikes, heated election contests and personality struggles are relevant, but this book is concerned with a deeper kind of conflict, one that reflects the day-to-day anxieties and aspirations of Illinois people as a whole. My intention is to get beneath the familiar events and unusual personalities to provide a description of the way ordinary people of Illinois have lived, and an interpretation of what they sought out of life. Mine will be a story of conflict and accommodation between groups of people at each stage of Illinois history—groups that differed in their fundamental values, in ways that help account for some of the more dramatic events and colorful leaders in Illinois history. I hope the reader might find here a deeper understanding of the state's people and of their significance in the history of America as a whole.

An analysis of the behavior of millions of people during a century and a half is risky, of course. It requires generalizations that cannot account perfectly for every case. Throughout this book, however, I will try to explain historical developments as reflections of general attitudes, using broad concepts that I believe have fundamental, if not universal, validity. I think that much can be understood about economics, politics, religion, and social and family life in Illinois and American history if one recognizes three different historical patterns of thought about life—basic sets of values, leading people to behave differently, that fall into three general categories: "traditional," "modern," and "postmodern."

The reader will have little trouble with these terms if he understands that I use them in a specialized sense, not the usual colloquial way. By "traditional," for example, I do not mean old or old-fashioned, though some element of that is involved. By "modern" I do not just mean recent or contemporary, and "postmodern" is not necessarily a reference to what will happen in the future.

These three terms are used to describe ways of thinking about life and styles of behavior. "Traditional" refers to a psychological outlook of people who are comfortable with things as they were, who distrust strangers and progress for progress's sake. The traditionalist prefers to rely on kinfolk and favors strong, masculine authority figures, such as the father within the family, the priest in religion, or the boss in politics. The first two chapters show that traditionalism was dominant among the earliest pioneers in southern Illinois, and among later arrivals such as Roman Catholic immigrants and blacks. To be sure, traditionalism in Illinois was never so extreme as in some peasant societies in the world, but it did stand in sharp contrast—and, often, in bitter conflict—with "modernity."

"Modern" refers to the future-oriented, upwardly mobile, reformist Yankees who came to the state before the Civil War, as well as to their imitators in the nineteenth and twentieth centuries. The "modern" person emphasizes efficiency, progress, independence, education, science, technology, and, especially, strict self-disciplined internal motivation, as against values rooted in family loyalty or religious authority. By the 1970s many characteristics associated with the "modern" outlook had been prominent for more than a century and were beginning to seem downright old-fashioned; but they were still distinct from "traditionalism."

Modern values are now falling into disrepute because of the emergence in the 1960s and 1970s of a "postmodern" outlook, especially among younger people. They downplay the ideals of progress, efficiency, and growth for growth's sake in favor of a search for more personal freedom and for more social equality (as opposed to equality of opportunity, which is a distinctly "modern" value). The postmodern person is suspicious of authority, alienated from the "establishment," and inclined to experiment with drugs, sex, and the occult. Equipped with a modern education and saturated with affluence, the postmodern person is unwilling to accept modern ideals or return to the narrow provincialism of the traditionalists. Readers puzzled as to why I did not make fuller use of familiar guideposts such as liberalism, urbanization, industrialization, the Protestant ethic, and class deserve an explanation. In my opinion, most of the usefulness of these ideas can be incorporated into the modern-traditional framework. "Liberalism," for example, was a useful label in politics from the 1930s to the 1960s to describe supporters of the New Deal, strong labor unions, government regulation, and welfare programs. Most liberals were Democrats and vice versa. The conservatives opposed liberal policies and high taxes, and tended to favor business. Conservatives were normally Republicans, and vice versa. It can be seen that liberals were basically concerned with helping people they considered the victims of modernization—the poor, the old, the unemployed, consumers, workers, and later, blacks. They wanted to use government to help these "minorities" become more modern. The conservatives feared that liberal programs would slow down or (in the case of reverse discrimination) even stop the progress of modernization. Although useful in interpreting domestic politics, the terms *liberal* and *conservative* meant little in foreign policy debates. It is possible to trace the origins of liberalism before the New Deal; I have not done so because I feel this is more a matter for an intellectual and political history on a national scale than for a book on Illinois. After the mid-1960s, the liberal-conservative distinction became less meaningful even in politics, since most of the battles occurred within the respective camps. The fight for control at the 1968 and 1972 Democratic national conventions was between older liberals (Daley, Humphrey) and younger rebels. Similarly the struggle between Ford and Reagan advocates in 1976 split the conservative ranks in the Republican party.

Urbanization implies modernization in most developing countries, as well as in the American South. This correlation did not hold in Illinois, where rural areas and small towns often took the lead. Today, for example, agriculture is the most progressive sector in the Illinois economy. The people of a state can become modern without benefit of big cities, as the farm states west of Illinois prove. Conversely, a glance at ghetto conditions in Chicago and East Saint Louis proves that living in the metropolis does not automatically produce modern lifestyles. Likewise, industrialization can be a misleading concept in a state where agriculture is very much a modern industry—and the largest one to boot—and where most twentieth-century growth has come in white collar and service jobs rather than factory employment. Obviously urbanization has occurred in Illinois, but I am arguing that the interplay of values and behavior was a psychological and social phenomenon that did not depend on the size of a place a person lived in.

The ''Protestant ethic'' is sometimes used by historians of the nineteenth century to describe what I call modern values. The term is highly misleading because only some Protestants, especially Methodists, Presbyterians, and Congregationalists, were leaders in modernization, but groups like German Lutherans and Baptists clung to traditional values much longer. True, Catholics were much more traditional than most Protestants before World War II. Since then, however, they have become equally if not more modern. Jews in Illinois quickly emerged as a very modern group. The Spanish element in Illinois (equally of Puerto Rican or Mexican descent) remains quite traditional, though given their shorter tenure in the state there is every indication they will modernize rapidly.

The reasons for using modernization rather than class to unify this book are more complex. From the mid-nineteenth century to the 1950s, the distinction between middle and working class conforms fairly well to the modern-traditional distinction. However, Illinois farmers do not fit into a class analysis. As late as the 1920s half the people in Illinois had been reared on farms, and their upbringing was critical even when they had migrated to towns or cities. To speak of their class origins would not be helpful. Farmers, however, can be classified as more modern or traditional by looking at their integration into the market economy, their use or avoidance of technology, their attitude toward education and reform, together with their religious values. Furthermore, one of my chief concerns has been the process by which some town and farm boys became middle-class, white-collar workers, and others became working-class, blue-collar

workers. I have examined this problem in detail elsewhere,[1] but
have incorporated some of the findings here. Something prior to
and more important than class has to be used to explain class.

The connotations of familiar terms easily produce misunder-
standing. The use of class terminology inevitably scares up
Marxist interpretations based on an inherent conflict between the
working-class proletariat and capitalists. No historian has been
able to use Marxism to interpret anything in Illinois history besides strikes. Most people use Marxist terminology to whip up
crowds, one way or the other. Neither Marxist nor anticom-
munist rhetoric seems especially useful in understanding the history of this state.

Class analysis does not explain developments since World
War II satisfactorily. The working-class population in Illinois
rapidly adopted middle-class values, ranging from faith in education, heightened nationalism, personal lifestyles, even distrust
of politicians. Meanwhile the more established middle class
abandoned much of the intense self-discipline so characteristic
of modernity. Charge-account lifestyles, the quest for luxury
and new experiences, freer sexual standards, full-time careers
for women, and a lesser concern with efficiency are notable ex-
amples. The children of the privileged middle class moved dramatically since the 1960s toward imitating certain lower-class
lifestyles so that age, more than anything else, divided the population. Today, therefore, Illinois is home for traditionalists,
moderns, and postmoderns.

The clashes in Illinois among the three groups illuminate the
nature of the American character. The advantages of seeing Illinois as a microcosm of the nation were appreciated as early as
1830 by one perceptive visitor, who reported that the inhabitants
of the state "are a complete mixture of almost every class of
civilized men, from every part of the United States. And this I
consider a most happy circumstance, not only because it is
highly improving to associate with persons of different habits
and modes of thinking, and from different parts of the world,

---

1. Richard Jensen and Mark Friedberger, *Education and the Modernization of the
Midwest* (Cambridge: Harvard University Press, 1978).

but because it is the most effectual method to destroy forever all local prejudices and groundless preferences, to discover the folly of an unreasonable attachment to long-established customs, and to promote general good feelings and liberality of sentiment.''

Illinois

1

Pioneer Traditionalism, 1800–1840

ILLINOIS was a place of escape, not a land of hope for its first American settlers. In the half-century after the American Revolution, tens of thousands of pioneers poured across the Appalachian Mountains into the fertile lands of Kentucky, Tennessee, Ohio, and Indiana. As white numbers grew exponentially from phenomenally high birth rates and continuous emigration from the eastern seaboard, and the thin lines of outnumbered, outgunned Indians fell back, the frontier pushed westward. By 1810 large numbers of settlers began arriving in southern Illinois. Easy lines of travel westward along the Ohio and northward along the Wabash, Mississippi, and Illinois rivers made it simple to reach the new land. The gentle hills and fertile river valleys of southern Illinois teeming with game seemed like the land of Canaan—though in time pioneers began to call the land "Egypt."

Little stood in the way of this new influx of people. A few thousand Indians of the Illinois and related tribes pursued a seminomadic way of life in the area that would be named for them. Frenchmen who came to explore and trap beaver appeared in the seventeenth century, and, though never numerous, established small settlements along the rivers. Both Indians and French fled under pressure from the incursion of American pioneers flooding into the land in the early nineteenth century. The French and Indian heritage thus consisted of little more than place names, like "Illinois" itself, and "Chicago," "Peoria," and "Vermillion."

By 1818, when Illinois became a state, some 4,600 families had arrived; by 1830 the number had jumped to 40,000. The great majority of pioneers in Illinois were southerners, men and women of Scotch-Irish or English descent who previously had lived in Kentucky, Tennessee, the Carolinas, or Virginia. These pioneers were scarcely wealthier than their poverty-stricken ancestors who came to America between 1630 and 1750 as settlers or indentured servants.

The lifestyle, values, and beliefs of the Illinois pioneers closely resembled those of their relatives and compatriots nearby in Indiana, Kentucky, Tennessee, and Missouri, or, for that matter, back in the Carolinas. One important difference must be emphasized. Illinois had only a few slaves tolerated as holdovers from the French regime or kept as household "servants" indentured for life. To the south, slavery was a major fact of life—Kentucky counted 127,000 slaves in 1820, as against 917 in Illinois. The absence of plantation slavery did not mean Illinois was an abolitionist haven, far from it, but it did mean that no large, rich, articulate slaveowner class existed to dominate society, economy, and politics. Indeed, many Illinois settlers were poor yeoman farmers who had been squeezed or cheated off good land in Kentucky or Tennessee by aggressive, profit-minded slaveowners. Since the states north of the Ohio River lacked slave codes to control the blacks, catch runaways, and make these human chattels safe investments, the slaveowners made no effort to move in, buy up large parcels of the choicest land, and establish their "peculiar institution" as they were doing in Missouri.

The poverty-stricken young men and women who settled Illinois brought with them distinctive customs and values—some of which can be traced back to Elizabethan England, others of which were forged in the generations of hardships, adventures, and struggles that were their American heritage. We will refer to the values which shaped their lives as "agrarian traditionalism." The term "traditionalism" distinguishes them from the "modernizers"—Yankees mostly—who arrived a little later in Illinois and who will be covered in the next chapter.

"Agrarian" simply means that the pioneers depended on subsistence agriculture, doing without much in the way of technology, cities, or money. This reliance on farming contrasts with the urban traditionalism exemplified by the Catholic immigrants who began arriving in the 1840s, or the blacks who immigrated mostly in the twentieth century.

Traditionalism can be understood in terms of two related values, masculine supremacy and intense, parochial loyalty to a narrow circle of people: self, family, kinfolk, perhaps the church congregation, and certainly to the white race. The family, and frontier society generally, was organized by and for the benefit of men. Perhaps it was inevitable in dangerous times; people often said the frontier was easy for men and horses, hard for women and oxen. Morality found expression in the parochial masculine loyalties. Fighting, lying, and stealing were acceptable to the extent they enhanced loyalties, and reprehensible only if they weakened them. One loyalty that developed slowly, and then only under drumbeats of war, or in the face of coercion, was loyalty to the state and obedience to the letter and spirit of the law.

Since few pioneers belonged to churches, let alone any other organization that might broaden their outlook on man, society, or nature, superstition and fatalism shaped their understanding. Men of science occasionally passed through Illinois, observing the flora, fauna, and geology; only a handful of trained physicians tarried long. Whether folk remedies were as dangerous as the harsh purgatives and routine bleedings of the doctor cannot be said, though illness was frequent, sudden death a common visitor. Without technological, scientific, or intellectual tools to overcome the forces of nature, the pioneer could only be fatalistic. Planning for the future did little good; it seemed better to live day by day, letting fate and luck decide what would happen. Gambling was wise when a man felt lucky; courage in skirmishes with the Indians was easier to muster once it was realized that mysterious fate, more than discipline and caution, arbitrated life and death in the forest. The favored religious sect on the frontier made fatalism a credo of theology in the guise of predestination. They "preach the hardest election doctring that I ever heard," explained one perplexed observer. "They say they were created for Heaven (the church members) and such as die in their sins were created for Hell.''

The pioneer was not afraid of change as such, nor was he wedded to the past, for he lacked a richly textured lifestyle filled with ancient traditions, fixed customs, colorful pageantry or powerful castes of priests and aristocrats. Rather, he was an individualist, alone against the world. To protect his family he did not form voluntary societies or petition for a redress of grievances. He loaded his rifle, or he fled. Had not the rich in Kentucky controlled the government as they seized more land and threatened the yeoman with the fate of becoming a "white nigger"? Better to move on to an unhealthy, unfamiliar land that at least promised complete liberty to the poor man. In Illinois one could be as carefree as he wished (if alert to Indians), without constantly fretting about unfair taxes, unpaid debts, old feuds, and unscrupulous land stealers.

Illinois was thus "the land of rest to the weary, the place of refuge to the oppressed.'' The traditionalist pioneers showed little sense of material ambition for themselves or their children. They "do the least work I believe of any people in the world,'' noted one traveller. Another found them "destitute of any energy or enterprise . . . their labors and attentions being chiefly confined to the hunting of game . . . and tilling a small batch of corn for bread.'' That, at least, was a misinterpretation: most of the corn became whiskey. Wealth was more often produced by gambling, land speculation, or political corruption than by hard labor. Education was a useless frill for boys and girls both; better they learn loyalty and how to fight. The children might be better off when they grew up—if they grew up—or they might not. Fate would decide that.

Yet the vagaries of fate were resisted by men, who made all the important decisions on the frontier. They saw their duty to protect their family from the infinity of dangers lurking about. They would fight to protect their honor and their family, and to keep strangers away. The women were smaller, were weaker, and often were pregnant or nursing babies. The men were stronger and used their muscle to slap around an impudent wife or whip a sassy child. The abused wife might flee back to her parents or run off with another man; more likely she took her punishment because she and the children were helpless without a man. Only masculine qualities were celebrated on the frontier—brute strength, raw courage, recklessness, heavy drinking, expert marksmanship. Only the men were allowed the favorite pastimes of interminable hunting and fishing trips, long bouts of heavy drinking, rough fighting, swearing, and boasting. Feminine virtues of tenderness or spontaneous affection were for sissies.

In their flight for freedom, the pioneers left behind any respect they might have had for abstract codes of law, authority, or hierarchy outside their extended family. They had escaped the tight-knit social and political cliques that totally controlled local government in the South and were in no humor to see the same evils reappear in Illinois. Nor would they doff their coonskin caps to any squires, slaveowners, or politicians; they had no truck with paternalism or deference politics. Respect for laws and courts, consequently, was weak. Lynch law, enforced by bands of neighbors and relatives was often the only way to deal with marauding Indians, horsethieves, or villains. Politics was highly personalized, built on favors and kinship connections rather than on issues. Individualism and equalitarianism meant something on the Illinois frontier: it meant freedom to express the particularistic loyalties of the traditionalist ethos.

No matter how carefree the pioneer wished to be, just getting to Illinois and setting up a farmstead did require a little effort. Anyone too lazy could remain in the hills and backlands of Appalachia. Of course, a man who underestimated the trouble involved in pioneering could always go back, and many did. Movement westward came in short leaps, perhaps fifty or a hundred miles at a time, with a new move every few years for the younger folk. The more foresighted settler would scout out the land, consult with kinfolk who had moved ahead, then select a likely spot. Prairie land was unsuitable—it was too much work to break the sod, haul in lumber for shelter and fuel, and find good water. Besides, soil that did not grow tall trees was not considered to be very fertile. The best location would be forest land, with a clear stream on it and not far from a river. No matter that it was hilly: that just made it more like home. In fact, the prairie soil was extremely rich. Traditionalistic farmers, however, showed little ingenuity in dealing with new, technical problems when it was easier to cling to the old ways. Thus southern pioneers concentrated in Egypt, that is, the lower third of the state, plus some river valleys farther north, leaving to the Yankees the challenge of taming the prairies. Most land was owned by the federal government, which never evicted squatters. Private land, however, might be better situated and even have a clearing and a cabin already prepared. For $2 or $3 an acre, the settler with some cash could do "right well." In any case it was wise to clear a few acres and plant some corn the summer before the big move.

Few of the traditionalists invested the time to plan thoroughly. They just "upped and moved," trekking overland to Vincennes, Shawneetown, or Kaskaskia before plunging into the wilderness. A North Carolina man, lugging westward all his possessions in 1835, was asked where he was heading. "No where partick'lar," he allowed. "Me and my wife thought we'd hunt a place to settle. We've no money, nor no plunder—nothin' but just ourselves and this nag—we thought we'd try our luck in the new country."

The migrants were young people, newlyweds with their few possessions loaded on a pony, or couples in their late twenties or early thirties who needed a cart to carry the ax, kettles, clothing, and children they had accumulated at the last stop. A crude lean-to provided shelter from the frequent rains and scorching sunshine of southern Illinois. Often it served for a year or more before the pioneer got around to raising a log cabin with the help of neighbors. To make a go of forest farming, five or ten acres had to be cleared of trees and underbrush. Big thick trees would be girdled and cut later, or maybe just ignored. A crude plow, pulled by oxen, could be hired for turning the soil the first time, breaking the old roots that had to be cleared. After that, however, plowing could be done more easily. Corn was always the first crop. In virgin soil it might yield twenty-five to fifty bushels to the acre with indifferent cultivation. In the lush Mississippi River bottom land, across from Saint Louis, 100 bushels was common.

Before the first harvest, the pioneers lived off game. Masculine hunting skills proved vital to survival—though a steady diet of deer, pheasant, and rabbit cooked without salt was monotonous. The first crop of corn, however, could be ground by hand into meal for johnnycakes. It would also feed the horse, the cow, and pigs that might carelessly happen by. Much of the corn found its way to a neighbor's still, where a seventy-five-gallon year's supply of drinking whiskey could be distilled from an acre of grain. After a few years of corn the soil was ready for wheat, which made a much tastier flour, assuming there was a gristmill not too far away.

After breaking in a few acres, the pioneer could relax. It took only forty or fifty days a year to plow, plant, cultivate, and harvest ten acres of corn; half that time for wheat. In fair weather, which held most of the time, it was coon hunting season, or perhaps the catfish were biting. Otherwise the family could huddle inside the small dirt-floored, leaky cabin and set the dogs to tease the pigs. In case boredom threatened, a man could clean his rifle or whittle a stick or, better, taste to see how well the "likker" had aged.

Ambition and devotion to hard work were neither prized traditional qualities, nor were they of much use to the backwoods farmer. Time was measured by seasons, not with calenders or clocks, for there never were schedules or deadlines to meet. There was little market for his goods, even if he did raise a surplus. Saint Louis was the only city of any size within easy distance of southern Illinois, and there were no nearby cities to the south or east that needed grain. Home-brew whiskey fetched low prices and could not compete at a distance with fine Kentucky bourbon or Tennessee mash. It was possible to raise cattle and hogs and drive them to a riverport for shipment south; most farmers who experimented with this practice lost money. Without markets, only subsistence agriculture was feasible. Naturally, money was scarce—the pioneer often saw no currency for months at a time. A smart horse trade, or sale of supplies to newcomers, netted the cash occasionally needed for land purchase or taxes.

Tax collectors had little work to do—and probably even the little proved unpleasant. The 117 households in Johnson County owed $200 in assessment in 1818—$15 from three taverns, $114.50 from a 50-cent tax on the 229 horses there, and $9 from a head tax on the nine slave families. A penny-an-acre tax on land yielded $50 for the state treasury. The revenue paid the sheriff's salary of $50 and the clerk's salary of $30 (they also received fees for various duties, like serving arrest warrants or issuing marriage licenses), with the surplus available for miscellaneous expenses and for repayment of the new county's $2,000 debt. "Poor little Johnson," sighed the county clerk. "But," he brightened, "it is not yet on the Parish" (meaning it had not been reduced to receiving charity).

The traditionalists who "suckered" the land by planting corn and wheat every year without fallowing it soon discovered the soil was worn out. A little rest and manure might restore it; more likely it appeared to be time to move on to a better place. The migratory habits that brought the pioneer to Illinois could just as well carry him off again. About a third of the 4,600 families in the state in 1818 left within two years, while another 4,000 or 5,000 moved in. This high rate of turnover was, however, not unusual by nineteenth-century standards. Nor, for that matter, would it be especially high in today's urban world.

The newcomers who had cash naturally preferred a well-located farm already partly cleared and provided with a cabin. Their payment gave the sellers some money with which to move westward. The new settlers, though but slightly more ambitious than the pioneers, cleared more timber and enlarged the cabin, thus slowly developing the land. Growth in the farm population naturally fostered the growth of tiny villages, which soon became centers of trade and entertainment. Villages that became county seats—perhaps after a stiff competition—had a fair chance to emerge as towns. In 1819, an uninhabited tract of land was selected as the site for the state capital, and so Vandalia appeared and soon became a thriving town of a few hundred. Few hunters or farmers moved to the towns, however. The lawyers, merchants, artisans, and laborers came from different backgrounds.

The interiors of the tiny pioneer cabins were typically as bleak as the exterior. The cabin walls were logs, chinked with mud to keep out the wind. The floor was usually dirt, and heat came from a smoky fireplace. "Many a rich farmer lives in a house not half so good as your old hog pen and not any larger,'' wrote a New Salem man to his family in New Hampshire in 1834. John Mason Peck, a Baptist missionary and keen observer, gave a picture of a ''fair specimen'' of hundreds of frontier farms in 1818. A small log cabin in the middle of the cornfield housed an old man, his wife, a grown son, a grown daughter, and two married daughters with their husbands and three or four small children. Not a table, chair, or bed cluttered the dirty cabin. ''Shiftless indeed,'' thought Peck, ''and void of all backwoods' skill and enterprise, who could not make a table.'' A slab split from a large log and hewn down to a plank, fitted with peg legs, would have sufficed. Peck's host substituted a box, covered with a spread ''that might have answered any other purpose than a table cloth.'' Long hunting knives constituted the tableware. As the guest of honor, Peck was provided with the cracked earthen plate and the broken dirty fork. The missionary could hardly have anticipated better fare than his rancid bacon, half-cooked snap beans, good boiled corn, and sour buttermilk that was ''no go,'' as he put it. Not for naught did the travelling missionary preach that cleanliness was next to godliness.

Many pioneers, to be sure, lived a little more gracefully. But it is a false myth to attribute a golden age of arts and crafts to the early settlers. Their craftsmanship was limited to the bare necessities of life, and they showed little inventiveness or ingenuity—seldom were they able to maintain the skills they had learned as children back East. Clothing, until the 1830s, was nearly all handmade. Dressed deerskins covered many. Spinning wheels and looms were hard to carry and expensive to buy. Families that owned them could expect many tedious hours of cleaning and carding wool, spinning fiber into yarn, dyeing yarn, and weaving cloth. Small children wore simple long shirts. Women's dresses were hardly more elaborate, usually consisting of long frocks with straight sides and attached sleeves. Men wore straw hats, cotton shirts, and sturdy jeans. Underwear was unknown, and most people went barefoot or wore deerskin moccasins in the summer, and shuffled about in crude homemade shoes in winter. Warm boots were the luxury of the rich. Soap could be made from ashes, though its use was not noticed very much by early travellers. Bathtubs were unknown; privies were pretentious.

Poor frontiersmen fashioned their tools and utensils from the plentiful supply of wood about them. Spoons, bowls, cradles, yokes, and buckets were carved by hand. Pewter plates, tin cups, forks, and other eastern luxuries were expensive. The lucky family with some spare cash could buy them from travelling peddlers and could get them repaired every so often by itinerant tinners who could solder practically anything together. A sharp blade for knife or ax was beyond the ken of the handful of pioneer blacksmiths—better, they thought, to buy an eastern model. Good rifles were very expensive to import, but the locally crafted ones had the dangerous habit of bursting on a deer hunt. A day's trek to the nearest village permitted a man to barter some whiskey, pigs, or produce for lead and gunpowder, salt, candle molds, and new whiskey jugs.

Apart from the mental outlook of the pioneer, a crucial environmental factor impeded his progress: disease. Illinois was considered very unhealthy. New arrivals could soon expect to fall sick, and many died before they were fully established. The crude housing might have offered protection from Carolina winters, but it was inadequate for Illinois. Hundreds died in the bitter winter of 1830–1831. The settlers suffered from frequent exposure, a lack of hygiene, unbalanced diets, a rudimentary knowledge of healing skills, and endemic malaria. In large stretches of the new land, as late as the 1840s, virtually everyone was infected with malaria, or ague. The disease followed a curious course. In the fall, just before harvest time, one or more family members began showing symptoms—fever, violent shakes, chills; the next day the patient would feel normal, and the symptoms appeared again on alternate days. Quinine was known to help, but it was too scarce and expensive for most sufferers. Usually the ague spells would cease in a few days, to recur the following year or perhaps skip a year before striking again. The disease was seldom fatal, though its debilitating effects could weaken a person enough for other diseases to kill him. The best opinion held that poisonous vapors, especially along river bottoms, caused ague. Not until most swampland had been drained and the mosquito menace curbed did scientists discover the true cause. By the 1870s, malaria had ceased to be a major health threat in the state, though old-timers still suffered greatly from recurrence of the "Illinois shakes." Typhoid, or "brain fever," apparently was widespread in the early days, usually as a dangerous complication of malaria.

Other dread diseases, such as cholera and smallpox, struck in sudden epidemics in Illinois and throughout the country. More peculiar to the state was milk sickness, a deadly poisoning later traced to a certain plant. Cancer, stroke, and heart disease, the chief killers of modern times, were unknown, or at least undiagnosed in early times. Tuberculosis, which was the chief cause of death in the late nineteenth and early twentieth centuries, was but a minor factor in the first third of the 1800s.

Life expectancy at birth is not known for the frontier, but it probably ranged from forty-five to fifty years. This does not mean that people died in their forties. On the contrary. The infant death rate was high on the frontier, though probably not quite as high as in Europe or the rest of the world. Pregnant women were well fed in Illinois, so premature births were probably less frequent. Of 100 babies born in a year, perhaps 25 or 30 would never reach age five. The unlucky ones died from influenza, pneumonia, and intestinal disorders, usually within a few months of birth. The high mortality strengthened the sense of fatalism. "We never expect to raise any of our children," sighed a respected physician, "at least, till they are seven or eight years old." Once a child had passed the dangerous years, he could expect to live almost as long as anyone today. The future life expectancy of a person aged ten was about fifty more years; at age thirty, another thirty-five years could be planned on. The outlook for males and females was about the same. The risk to a woman of dying in childbirth, especially if no midwife was available, was matched by the man's higher risk of hunting and work accidents.

Male dominance on the frontier produced sex roles quite unlike those prevalent today. Men controlled all decisions, both within the household and among outsiders. Women had no clearly defined sphere of influence, no matter how small, in which they could make independent decisions. Not even the choice of marriage partners was free. To be sure, it was rare to find the sort of arranged marriages common to peasant societies in which the parents make the match without consulting the children. On the other hand, the sparse population of the frontier and the practice of churches prohibiting members from marrying those of other denominations severely limited the choice of eligible spouses. No matter how the couple came together, the bride's father (or brother or uncle) had to give his permission to marry. Elopement was possible, but rare. To get the bride's family's permission and protect its honor, the groom had to post bond. (With little cash in circulation, he simply obtained the signature on a guarantee bond from his father or a friend.) With a license from the county clerk, the marriage took place quickly, and a chivaree, or bawdy wedding night teasing of the newlyweds, sealed the union.

Dowries were very rare on the frontier, apart from the feather-bed, clothes, and surplus household items the wife might bring with her. Although illegitimate births were rare, shotgun marriages also seem to have been uncommon. More likely the reverse took place, with the bride getting pregnant to force her father's permission. "I reckon I'll approve," noted one father on the license, "seeing how far things have gone." We can attribute this pattern less to the sense of morality than to the practical situation. A man needed a wife and children. "A bachelor has no business in the Backwoods," it was said. "Imagine the uncomfortableness of inhabiting a log-cabin, where one is obliged to cut wood, clean the room, cook one's victuals, etc. etc." Likewise, a woman needed protection in a world where men controlled everything. In 1820 in Illinois, there was only one case recorded in the census of a single woman trying to maintain a household without a man around.

Within the marriage the husband ruled supreme in all matters. To underscore this relationship, the newlyweds moved immediately to their own house, thus escaping the control of the parents. If land for a new farm was not available nearby, the newlyweds headed toward the frontier. "We were married and came here to live," recalled a pioneer in Bond County. "We didn't *move,* for we had nothing to move. I had an old horse, cow, plow, and some home-made tools, and my wife had some household goods she had made. We had little money but did not need much, as we raised or made all we used." Production and consumption, in a subsistence economy, were not separated. The husband controlled both. In the spring and autumn planting and harvest seasons, all family members worked together in the fields, under the husband's supervision. Boys and girls were expected to turn out for field work from the age of six or seven, and by their mid-teens would be considered full hands. In less hectic times, the children played all they wanted. Inside work, such as preparing food and making clothing, was mostly done by women, while the men and boys hunted and fished. Both sexes tended the animals, and women did the milking. At all times it was clearly the husband who decided what was to be done, and when, how, and who should do it.

The wife's role in decision-making was wholly passive. If conditions became unbearable, however, she might run away. A pioneer in McDonough County, near Peoria, recalled that in 1829 the Indians were still numerous, and often came to their isolated cabin. His wife was terrified of them and begged to return to their earlier homestead twenty miles farther south. Since protection of the family was so clearly his function, the husband refused. Twice while he was away she packed all the household goods, but he returned too soon for her to get away. The third time she had the loaded wagon and two small children as far as the county line before being intercepted. This time she absolutely refused to return, and the family moved south. Four years later, when McDonough County was more heavily settled and the Indians had been expelled, the husband managed to convince her to move back with him. A half-century later the man stated he never regretted the return, though what the wife thought we do not know.

Couples normally married a few years younger on the frontier than they did in settled areas. The easy availability of free land meant there was little need to accumulate a nest egg of savings, nor was the prospect of a larger family disturbing to men whose children soon paid their keep. Men would marry about twenty-three, women about twenty, give or take two or three years. Despite folklore to the contrary, girls of fifteen or sixteen rarely were wed. The fertility of frontier marriages was astonishingly high—indeed, the highest the world has ever seen apart from frontier French Canada in the seventeenth century, and small colonies of intensely religious Hutterites today. From age twenty-one to her early forties, a woman could expect a baby every other year, for an average of ten in all. Contraceptive practices, like withdrawal, did not suit the masculine image of the husbands. Abortion and infanticide were probably practiced by a few unwed mothers. Thirty years after the marriage, half the families were still intact. Of the ten children born, seven would still be alive, with the oldest married off and the younger ones still helping out around the farm. In one-sixth of the marriages, the wife died and the widower promptly remarried, usually to a younger woman who might bear her own quota of ten children. In one-fourth of the marriages, the husband died. The widow, if she were under thirty, would probably remarry. After that age, however, she was not considered an eligible partner. If the children were strong enough, she could rear them by herself. Or she could return to her family. In one marriage in twelve, both spouses died before thirty years had passed. The older orphans—say, age fifteen and up—could make a go at the world themselves. They would not try to maintain the old family, however. The younger children needed adult supervision and were adopted by relatives. In the unhappy case where no relatives could adopt the orphans, local government would intervene. Willing families would take in the toddlers and be paid from the poor fund. Older children would be apprenticed as farmers, artisans, or servants. In a society without orphanages that was all that could be done. Indeed, it was a humane solution.

Frontiersmen took few special pains in rearing their children. Boys learned to hunt and farm by watching their fathers and following orders. Girls likewise acquired their skills from their mothers. Seldom did parents provide systematic training or assign routine chores. Indeed, given the large number of siblings frontier children lived with, it seems likely they learned more from their peers than from their parents. The result was that skills, especially craftsmanship, tended to deteriorate sharply on the frontier. Formal learning was, of course, quite useless under the conditions that prevailed. What use was reading in a land without books, or of arithmetic in a subsistence economy where barter had replaced cash sales? The proudest literary attainment in most cabins came in painfully formed signatures. Even the census takers, supposedly literate officials, had trouble spelling common names, as lists of "Bengman" (Benjamin), "Elexander," "Matha" (Matthew), and "Izrel" or "Isrual" testify. The spelling of the respectable frontier name Shadrach ("Shedrick," "Shaderick," "Shadric," "Chad") proved baffling to the orthographers of 1820.

Occasionally an itinerant teacher appeared in the backwoods, offering to exchange a little "learning" for his keep. Since food was cheap, and another body squeezed onto the floor could only make the cabin warmer in the winter, the farmers with a bit of ambition for their children pooled their resources for a few months. A child might thus obtain some rudimentary skills in the three Rs, or at least in either spelling or ciphering. The teachers were invariably men—perhaps a penniless New Englander, like Stephen Douglas, who needed a way to survive in the forest. Or a ne'er-do-well Irishman who would bear watching, but at least came cheap. The state owned vast school lands as a result of congressional action that set aside one section of every township for the support of schools; but not till the 1850s did public education begin. The Sunday schools set up by some churches in the 1820s might have provided a little learning, though the record shows they awarded their prizes to children who could memorize the greatest number of Bible and hymn verses.

The boy of the frontier wasted little energy acquiring skills that could not be used in his environment. What he did learn was that loyalty to family and kin was repaid with help in time of trouble; that strength and stamina could enable him to land his game or wrestle his opponent to the ground; that strangers meant trouble; that boys should always protect the girls; that if nearby land did not suit him, he could always push further westward. The child became the adult, imbued with traditionalist values now purified by exposure to a climate where deviation meant danger.

Old age was seldom a factor on the frontier. Only 2 percent of the population were over age sixty, only 8 percent were even forty-five years of age. Indeed, not for a century would there be enough old people to attract attention to their special needs. The dearth of aged was not, however, caused by excessively high death rates. Rather the frontier was settled by young couples, who did not become old till the time of the Civil War. By that time there would have been great numbers of their children and grandchildren and great-grandchildren, not to mention the enormous numbers of later settlers and their children. As a result, the elderly dropped from view. Peasant societies had a much greater proportion of old people, and important questions like land ownership and inheritance depended on the relationship between generations, but the few old people in early Illinois had no special role in society. They continued to farm their own lands, perhaps with the help of a son or a hired hand. The value of an inheritance was seldom important, for the land was cheap and the heirs were many.

No matter how isolated the pioneers seemed in their cabin, they did not have to face the wilderness alone. They could call upon an extended network of relatives for help in time of need. Morality was judged by the standards of the kinfolk, and in political matters all stood together. Close kin comprised parents, siblings, aunts and uncles, first cousins, nieces and nephews, and all their spouses and children. A man stood in special relationship to his wife, children, stepchildren and adopted children. The pioneer maintained equally close ties with his wife's close kin as with his own.

The implications of kinship became staggering when we recall the remarkably high fertility on the frontier. The average pioneer, at age forty-five, say, could count thirty or forty adult male brothers, brothers-in-law, and nephews—excluding uncles and first cousins. With the latter included, the number of adult male close kin might easily soar into the hundreds. Not to mention the men's own strapping teen-age children soon about to find mates for themselves. Of course, not all the kinfolk were in Illinois. Many lived back in Kentucky or North Carolina or Tennessee, while others had migrated to Indiana or pushed onward to Missouri, Arkansas, or points unknown. In a word, the typical family was not alone on the frontier. Sparse though the population might be, no matter where he found himself the pioneer was probably not far from a close relative who would be obligated to provide lodging, protection, and advice on call. Migration westward could thus be accomplished by a series of short moves punctuated by brief spells of visiting kinfolk. Thus a man near a main route could expect to see a lot of relatives coming and going, together with an occasional stranger every so often (the latter, of course, had to pay for his keep with cash). A wealthy Marylander en route to Saint Louis stayed with such a family in 1819: "At their dirty hovel, with one room and a loft, ten travellers slept. There were thirteen in the family, besides two calves, making in all, with my friend and myself, twenty-three whites, one negro and two calves. Supped on pumpkins, cabbages, rye coffee without sugar, bones of venison, salted pickles, etc.—all in the midst of crying children, dirt, filth and misery." Once one member of the family had established himself in Illinois and approved the place, word would spread quickly through the family network, and soon a cousin or nephew could be expected to settle nearby.

For routine communal activities, the relatives were too far-flung to bring together. Instead the pioneers depended on neighborhood gatherings. Cabin raising, cornhusking, logrolling, even hog-butchering was an occasion for a "bee." A half-dozen families would come together for a day, divide into work teams, and compete to see which could beat the others (it seemed less like labor that way). Heavy eating and drinking would follow, with the group ending the day by planning the next get-together. Women, usually pregnant or nursing babies, favored quilting bees; young people experimented with play parties and bussing bees. Serious courtship, however, took place before the girl's fireplace, with her siblings peeking. If the night was cold, the old practice of bundling warmed things up. Relations between neighbors were usually superficial. Unless the children intermarried, one family might migrate and never resume contact with its old neighbors. Stronger relationships focused on longer visits between relatives or on church involvements.

Court days and militia rosters brought everyone to town to watch the proceedings, drink, fight, race horses, shoot (at targets), or, if the mood was lively, have a gander pull. A live old gander was greased and its feet tied to a tree limb. Bareback riders had to race at the fluttering bird and snap its head off. If the gander failed to prove who the best man was, a wrestling match would settle the point. The contests were usually friendly affairs, testing brute strength and endurance rather than skills. A liquored-up rowdy or two might throw things out of control, with a hair-pulling, thumb-biting, face-scratching, kidney-kicking fracas that would fire up the crowd. The Illinois frontier won national fame for the skill of its eyegougers—though, to be fair, the short census list of blind men suggests there were fewer victims in fact than in legend.

Next to the group of kin, the church was the strongest force in the life of the individual—for those who belonged, that is. Few Americans, in the early nineteenth century, were church members. Only a fifth of the Illinois population were affiliated with churches, and they saw themselves as God's chosen people living in the midst of heathens. The Baptists were the most numerous group, with unlettered but enthusiastic preachers well suited to the ruggedness of the backwoods. The Methodists, with a brilliantly organized system of circuit riders, built the most successful network of churches. Their appeal was more to ambitious farmers and businessmen than to the fatalistic backwoods people. Newer sects, like the Campbellites (Disciples of Christ) and the Cumberland Presbyterians began to flourish a little later. Despite strenuous, well-financed missionary efforts, the sophisticated, well-educated Presbyterians attracted few converts. The Roman Catholics made little effort to proselytize, confining their energies to preserving the faith of growing Irish and German communities.

The traditionalist agrarian ethic meshed nicely with the plain, particularistic theology of the Baptists. The churches were quite small—perhaps only twenty families would belong to a congregation—and intensely inward-directed. Only men and women chosen by God for eternal salvation and suitably immersed in a formal baptismal ceremony could belong. The church was like a second family—the ministers were addressed as "Brother" and members were also called "brother" and "sister." The preacher, usually a neighboring farmer, or occasionally a travelling evangelist, would exhort his flock for hours, warning of the terrors of hellfire and promising his people a heaven that closely resembled a loafer's paradise. The Baptists were fiercely independent and carefully weighed the theological principles of other Baptist churches before extending fellowship to them. The Methodists were more centralized, with elected bishops and full-time paid circuit riders controlling every aspect of church development in pioneer days. Both groups, along with the Cumberland Presbyterians and Disciples, organized annual revivals to attract new members. Although these revivals most often caught the attention, and sarcasm, of outsiders, they were not at this time the central feature of frontier religion. Much more important was the bond of fellowship that existed inside the tight-knit congregation. The conviction of moral superiority—the sense of being one of God's chosen—provided the foundation for fellowship. It was maintained by weekly meetings, apart from the main religious service itself, that were as psychologically charged as encounter groups of the 1970s. The Methodist class meeting required a ticket from the minister for admission. It was limited to members and involved extemporaneous prayers, hymns, intense soul-searching confessions, even emotional outbursts. As the Methodist Church modernized, it abandoned class meetings in favor of revivals.

The frontier church people, especially the Baptists, closely monitored each others' morals, as well as their own. At weekly Baptist meetings a man might rise to confess he had gotten drunk or been in a fight, and then ask for forgiveness and a renewal of fellowship. It was usually given. However another member might accuse a man or woman of conduct unbecoming a Christian. A committee would investigate the charges and report its findings. If the accused was found guilty and did not show sufficient repentance—or worse, refused to co-operate—a vote of exclusion followed. A person who later repented might be readmitted, especially if the offense had been minor. The Baptists regularly expelled 1 or 2 percent of their members annually; some churches excluded up to half their members in a single year. Without a formal letter of good standing, a Baptist was unlikely to find another Baptist church that would accept him.

The church discipline records provide an invaluable guide to the state of morality on the frontier. By far the chief offenses were swearing, fighting, drunkenness, and nonattendance at meetings. However, all offenses came under the purview of the church morals courts. Gamblers, dancers, and Sabbath breakers were forced to mend their ungodly ways. Un-Christian behavior toward another member was a serious matter. A lawsuit against a fellow member was a grave violation of the spirit of intimate fellowship that sustained the congregation. Sharp business dealings against outsiders were also causes of complaint; it is interesting to note they seldom resulted in conviction. For example, one case involved a charge that the minister had exacted the regular rent from a tenant, even though the minister's livestock had destroyed the tenant's corn. Since the tenant was not a Baptist, and the minister had not violated the civil law, there was "no cause for complaint."

Excessive gossip was cause for a committee of inquiry, but the gravest and rarest cases involved sexual misconduct. Fornication and adultery, attempted or consummated, automatically brought expulsion—though one curious case involved a young woman who bore an illegitimate child. The case was dropped when she pointed out that conception had taken place before she was baptized. Her conversion had cleared away her sin, leaving only its now-innocent fruit. A newlywed who refused to sleep with her husband was expelled after two committees failed to make her understand her duty. On the other hand, a man who beat his wife too much was also liable to expulsion.

The greatest sins possible in a psychologically interdependent group involve deception and excessive pride. Heretics were expelled, no matter how harmless or pious, if they failed to accept the orthodoxy of the majority. A fraudulent minister was a terrible shock. In 1831 a Baptist church just across the Indiana line welcomed a preacher from South Carolina. He spent six months with the congregation, receiving its warmest thanks before setting off to Illinois. A month later the horrified Baptists discovered the man (John B. Smith, no less) was an "imposter." Furthermore, the record continued, "Said Smith has disgraced himself by repeated attempts at sodomy which can be sustained by evidence from within and without the Church." In a society that esteemed masculinity so highly, the people apparently had little familiarity with overt homosexuality. In any case, it is clear that Smith's sexual behavior was less cause for disgust or alarm than his fraudulent credentials.[1]

A majority of the pioneers, it should be emphasized, were not church members at all, and loyalty to the Word of God seldom figured in their reckoning. Their spiritual world encompassed not heaven, hell, and Christ crucified, but spirits, spells, and omens. While the Methodists and Presbyterians discouraged superstition, the Baptists were not so modern, seeing evil manifestations of the devil all about them. Eventually the frightening spirit world of the pioneers would be tamed, fit subjects for the entertaining folklore of oldtimers or, better, the immortal literature of Mark Twain's *Huckleberry Finn* (not Tom Sawyer—he was a modernizer!). Meantime, it was worth your sanity to sleep in the rays of a full moon, or to mess with old black women known to cast spells that would ruin a rifle's aim or make a cow give sour milk. While the nineteenth-century white pioneer was less fearful of the power of spirits than Indians, blacks, or Frenchmen, he remained on the alert against witchcraft. Hallowe'en was the most dreadful night of the year, scarier even than Friday the Thirteenth.

An elaborate folklore anticipated Ann Landers in providing guidance on important matters of everyday life. Horoscopes and "spirit-rapping" had not yet come into fashion, though astrological signs were noted with care and trepidation. The folklore was rich with advice and warnings. Root crops were best planted in the dark of the moon or when the zodiac was in the sign of the feet. Indian remedies, particularly medicinal herbs, were widely popular. Equally effective were persons possessed of mystical healing powers. The seventh son of a seventh son (a numerous tribe then, now all but extinct) was destined for special curative powers. Birthmarks were removed by rubbing

---

1. The status of homosexuals on the Illinois frontier is not clear. A search of church discipline records covering the morals of hundreds of men has turned up no other case. Travellers never comment on the matter, and historians have yet to survey enough court records to find instances (e.g., sodomy charges, divorce testimony). A scan of the 1850 census showed no case of two men living together alone; in 1818 and 1820, however, there were a dozen such pairs recorded. The cowboy frontier of a latter date and further west is a different matter.

thrice with the hand of a corpse or if none was available, with a live eel. Great care was required to protect infants. If mama cut his nails before nine weeks, her son would grow up a thief. A little bag containing the leg of a toad could ward off fits, and wearing the right forepaw of a mole was good for the croup. Horse chestnuts carried in the pocket would take care of piles; chicken soup—feathers and all!—could cure constipation. Dozens of other charms competed with the learned physicians' bloodletting in popularity.

The churches enhanced their cohesiveness by fostering marriages within the group. This actually widened the range of eligible spouses from immediate neighbors and "kissing cousins" to unrelated persons. The frontierspeople intermarried freely with natives of other states (except Yankees and foreigners, who rarely gave or took brides from their upland southern neighbors in Illinois). The dangers of genetic inbreeding were far below the level that later emerged in the incestuous Appalachians, and families enlarged their circle of helpful relatives much faster if cousins did not marry. Furthermore, a church member in good standing carried credentials of upright moral behavior that were otherwise impossible to obtain. A fellow Baptist could be trusted with one's daughter. Marriage to nonmembers was possible, but the churches frowned upon it. A Methodist who married a nonbeliever was put under close watch for six months. In-marriage strengthened the churches and made them more homogeneous. Eventually the Protestants relaxed their particularism, allowing marriage into any other Protestant denomination. Catholics, on the other hand, retained the traditionalistic practice of disapproving "mixed" marriages till the late twentieth century.

The overlap of church communities and family networks gradually permitted the diffusion of the churches' moral standards throughout southern Illinois. Every extended family came to contain a variety of church members—saintly, pious, quiet persons, successful men whose church connections proved advantageous, stern patriarchs or matriarchs who watched closely the behavior of hordes of nephews and nieces. Girls noticed that church member cousins seemed to make better matches; they were better provided for, less troubled by desertion and wife-beating, and apparently enjoyed a more active social life. In the drab monotony of pioneer life the revival camp meeting was the liveliest event women could participate in; periodically, the revivals touched off waves of conversions. In 1811, for example, the six Baptist churches in Illinois doubled their membership through conversions at revivals. A certain proportion (about one in four) of the new members lost interest and were soon excluded. The majority stayed and began entreating their relatives to come to the revivals. Thus church membership grew, and the moral influence of church discipline slowly became the community standard.

Although churches enrolled only a minority of the population, they set the tone of morality on the frontier. A person who passed intensive scrutiny every week enjoyed a favorable reputation. One who was expelled on charges that were soon widely known suffered public humiliation. No longer a saint, he was just another sinner. Only now he was depressed and lonely. Southern Illinois had a reputation for lawlessness and immorality that embarrassed the good god-fearing people of the region. When strict Yankees censored the southerners for their excessive enjoyment of the Sabbath, one inhabitant defended the morals of the land in 1848:

> The people of Egypt have sometimes been underrated because they have been dressed in homespun. It is true we have vice here and rustic vice, and yet we have not so much upstart infidelity as in some other apparently moral and religious communities. Many a person will shoot a deer or a turkey on a Sabbath and swear like a sailor when angry, drink a glass of grog with their neighbors, and run their horses a quarter for a wager, who would feel shocked at the thought of treating religion with disrespect or denying its divine origin.

The morality of the traditional pioneers was particularistic. Sin constituted an offense against God, to be sure, but in application it also meant an offense against the kinship group or the congregation. An action that brought turmoil or disgrace to the group was severely chastised—there was little sense of offense against the community at large. Rarely did the discipline meetings of the churches reflect on broader questions of morality. One exception occurred in 1833 when a man asked whether it was right to buy public lands without paying a squatter for the improvements he had made. After mulling the matter over for a month, the congregation decided it was not. On the other hand, church members were never chastised for cutting timber on public lands or on property owned by absentee speculators. When northern missionaries began establishing temperance societies to bring public pressure against excessive drinking, the Baptists split bitterly. Any moral policing agency outside the disciplinary procedures of the church was unacceptable to the traditionalists. When a Baptist church near New Salem expelled one member for drunkenness, and another for joining the temperance society, a puzzled member, rising excitedly to his feet and shaking the flask in his hand, demanded, "Now, brethering, how much of this critter have I got to drink to have good standing among you?"

The traditionalistic moral ethic did not look to the government as an arbiter of right and wrong. Law enforcement in Illinois was notably poor. In the river towns and mining camps (like the Galena lead mines or the salt works near Shawneetown), the coming together of rough, single men with money in their pockets brought prostitution, thievery, and counterfeiting on a large scale. Illinois was a favorite escape for desperados of all sorts. Occasionally, when the threat to peaceful settlers became severe, vigilante bands were formed. Some of those caught were hanged; most were brutally whipped.

The legal system was not well designed for the administration of justice. Jurors would not vote to convict kinsmen. Strangers could be convicted; though without secure jails or a state penitentiary the usual punishment was a fine or whipping. Murderers often won acquittals, received light sentences, or fled the state. Execution was rare. In Lawrence County only one person was hanged before the Civil War—Elizabeth Reed, who poisoned her husband in 1843. A rapist or a horsethief, if convicted, might expect fifty or sixty lashes, and a few days in jail or a $100 fine. Stephen Douglas was proud that as a judge he courageously fined a "notorious desperado" for beating his wife, and also freed the woman with a divorce. Despite angry threats, Judge Douglas was not injured. The courts seldom handled criminal matters. In McLean County only seven criminal cases appeared on the docket in 1838. However, the thousand families there originated no fewer than 368 civil cases that year. The courts served not as fairhanded dispensers of equal justice, but as devices by which men attacked their enemies. Charges of slander and fraud, buttressed with perjured testimony, were used to injure and humiliate an opponent. Often the cases dragged on for years, growing so complicated that the sharpest legal talents around were unable to finish them off and collect the last of their fees. Political and family feuds sometimes burst courtroom confinement and led to bloody vendettas.

The traditionalist settlers had vague notions of the role of government, except that it should rid the land of Indians. Back in Kentucky, Virginia, and the Carolinas, where strong, active local government was entirely in the hands of a self-perpetuating oligarchy, the pioneer had fared poorly. Illinois squatters were rarely forced off their lands, but the unpleasant memories did little to instill confidence in government.

The average settler had only a slightly larger role in Illinois government than in the older states. True, all adult white men could vote and usually did. In 1824, for example, three-fifths of the men voted for governor. However, seeking and holding office were the exclusive province of a select group of wealthy gentlemen, mostly Kentuckians. The class of politicians had genuine leadership skills, augmented by military and legal talents. They judged it their prerogative to govern, and used officeholding to gain honor and to obtain lucrative patronage and inside deals on land speculation. Elections brought the people together for heavy drinking, excited talk, fancy speechmaking, and the inevitable brawls. Politicians built their coalitions on the basis of friendship and favors with kin groups and local elites. Before the 1830s, issues rarely concerned the pioneer. He expected little favors, much whiskey, and an acknowledgment from the candidate that the people in this land were the salt of the earth, God's most noble creation. The politicians in turn were after government contracts, land, personal glory, and the power that patronage would give them. The keenest reporter in Vandalia, the state capital, felt "there never was a period in the history of our country, in which the public men have sought popularity, power, and office with so much avidity, or have shown so little scruple, as to the means by which their purposes might be effected.'' Local militia units often provided the leadership, and the voting blocs, in elections. The pioneers were good judges of leadership—that is, of the ability to talk loud, shoot straight, ride fast, give commands, and fear nothing. Voter turnout was light in presidential contests, for the governor, legislature, and county court had more to offer than the White House. Andrew Jackson, the hero of the southwestern militia in the War of 1812, and a great Indian fighter, dueller, and rugged exemplar of frontier masculinity, was one of the few national figures to elicit admiration on the frontier. His supporters, working through the militia, managed to form a coalition of politicians and voters that emerged as the Democratic party in the 1830s.

For the most part, the typical pioneer was content to be left alone by the government. Taxes were low, services were nonexistent, laws were few, and law enforcement spotty at best. Neighbors, not the sheriff, would attend to criminals. The big worry was that an enemy might sue in court and seize land or property. The best protection was to have a kinsman on the jury (everyone did, so juries rarely convicted anyone). Next best was to have an understanding with the lawyer-politicians who controlled the courts, so that, at worst, a man could get an honest hearing.

The pioneers did have two deeply held political sentiments: they loved liberty and hated aliens. The former was expressed mostly in exuberant Fourth-of-July celebrations till the new parties in the 1830s discovered ways to harness the holiday for less patriotic ends. The hatreds, born out of narrow vision and years of fighting British and Indians, were seldom put to the test. The mild-mannered French Catholics, who had inhabited villages along the Mississippi for a century, quickly gauged the spirit of the American pioneers and early fled for their lives to Missouri. The hapless few who remained were robbed, cheated, raped, beaten, and often killed. The Yankees who began arriving in large numbers in the 1830s were doubly suspect: not only did they represent an alien way of life, but they were ingenious in protecting themselves and were just as aggressive, though in subtler ways, as the southerners.

The traditional pioneers also hated and feared the Indians. Outnumbered and outgunned, the latter were driven from most of the territory by 1815, after an exchange of massacres. In 1832 Black Hawk, leading a breakaway faction of Sac Indians, attempted to recover lands near Rock Island he decided his tribe should not have sold to the Americans. The pioneers overnight rushed to arms and drove the Indians to slaughter in Wisconsin. Soon the last Indian titles were purchased by the government, and the white man reigned supreme in Illinois.

Supreme, but not alone, for blacks were always present. Slavery existed on a small scale from the French days to the 1840s, protected by an article in the 1818 constitution allowing indentured servitude. The salt works near Shawneetown employed hundreds of slaves imported temporarily from Kentucky. For a while in the 1810s and 1820s, the salt works was the largest industrial enterprise in the entire West. However, the salt lost its market to imports, and the operation and with it Illinois's short experiment with industrial slavery shrank into insignificance.

In 1824 the pioneers had an opportunity to make Illinois a slave state. Wealthy politicians, disappointed that so many slaveowners were taking their property across the state to settle plantations in Missouri, forced a referendum on calling a convention that would change the constitution and allow the "peculiar institution" to take root. No appeal was made that slavery was a good thing. Rather, settlers were encouraged to think a wave of slaveowner immigration would produce a sharp rise in land values. Opponents of slavery—all modernizers of a type we shall consider at length in the next chapter—were ineffective in their denunciation of slavery as a violation of the Declaration of Independence and of true morality. These opponents proved more effective in warning that slavery would cause thievery, threaten race war, and install the slaveowners as insufferable aristocrats who would lord over the common man. The referendum was narrowly defeated, and the threat that Illinois might become a slave state lay dormant until the Dred Scott decision of 1857 forced the issue to the center of political debate.

While traditionalists feared slavery, they also intensely opposed free blacks living in their midst. Special laws imposed harsh terms on the small black population. Free blacks were not allowed to vote, sue, testify in courts, serve in the militia, or enjoy free use of their property; they were also segregated. In the 1840s abolitionists tried to help slaves fleeing from Kentucky and Missouri escape to Canada. The "underground railway" worked poorly, however, and most runaways were caught, and some free men were kidnapped and shipped south as slaves. In 1853 the legislature forbade free blacks from entering the state; an effort in 1862 to enshrine this law in the state constitution nearly succeeded.

The agrarian traditionalism of the frontier cannot be considered some sort of transition stage between peasantry and modernity. It was a distinct lifestyle, shaped in part by external circumstances such as the lack of effective government, easy access to practically free land, and long years of battling Indians. To survive under these conditions, male supremacy and clan loyalty were essential. Colorful provincial costumes, hallowed customs, and devout rituals never constituted a part of the frontiersman's needs. The Illinois pioneer was no peasant: he controlled his own life, never bowed subserviently to a landed aristocracy, an established church, or an autocratic government. In casting off old customs, including deference to men of "superior" station, he lost some valuable skills (like handicrafts) and gained in return a new freedom in a new land.

Modern readers imbued with a profound respect for hard work, ambition, honesty, and the sanctity of the law will find the traditional pioneers strange and unpleasant folk, and will wonder if they perhaps compensated for their "faults" by contentment and happiness. Travellers found the pioneers glum, suspicious people, much given to melancholy, ill health, and miserable living conditions. But they were content when left alone, for they had succeeded in creating a society that reflected their innermost values, which did not seem to them to be in need of improvement.

In the 1830s the modernizers began arriving and discovered that everything needed reform in Illinois. They devoted the next century to establishing new standards, much to the distress of the outnumbered and ridiculed traditionalists. Yet from this conflict of cultures, from an extremely traditional family, in fact, emerged the outstanding spokesman of the nineteenth century for modern values in America, Abraham Lincoln.

2

The Modernizers Arrive, 1830–1860

LLINOIS was the fastest-growing territory in the world in the middle nineteenth century. Only 19th in size among the twenty-five states in 1830, with a mere 25,000 pioneer families, Illinois leaped to fourth place in 1860 with more than 300,000 families, then added another 160,000 families in the decade of the Civil War. That brought the total population to 2,500,000, with enough coming to double the population again by the end of the century. The new arrivals drove their teams and wagons across Ohio and Indiana, took passage on steamboats out of Buffalo or New Orleans, or, after the mid-1850s, swarmed through Chicago by rail.

"The fame of these fertile prairies has attracted here a greater variety of characters than is to be found in the neighboring states," noted a traveller as early as 1830. By 1870 Illinois was a heterogeneous society: 22 percent of the family heads had come from the Northeast; 14 percent—mostly old pioneers— were from the South; 27 percent came from the Midwest (including 12 percent who were native sons). The large balance were Europeans, chiefly British (8 percent), Irish (9 percent), and German (15 percent). Except that a mere 1 percent were nonwhite, Illinois had become a microcosm of the entire United States.[1]

The transformation of Illinois from a lazy man's paradise to a

1. The enthnicity data in this chapter come from a random sample of 1,116 households drawn from the original manuscript schedules of the 1870 federal census.

POPULATION in ILLINOIS · 1830 and 1860

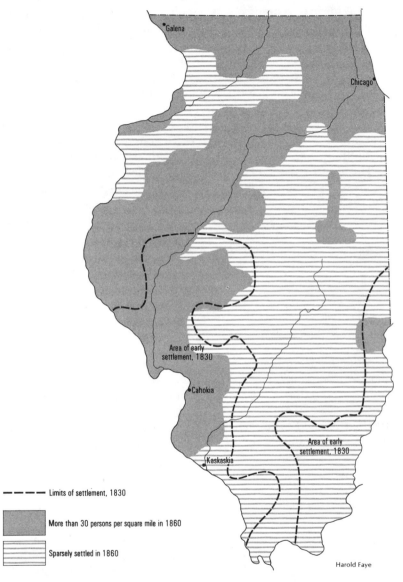

Galena

Chicago

Area of early
settlement, 1830

Cahokia

Area of early
settlement, 1830

Kaskaskia

— — — Limits of settlement, 1830

More than 30 persons per square mile in 1860

Sparsely settled in 1860

Harold Faye

dynamic modern society was neither accident nor inevitable fate. A new psychology was required, that of the modernizer. The men and women who brought it to Illinois came west to better themselves and to create a great society on the prairie. They took a poor outpost of traditionalism and transformed it into one of the richest, most progressive areas anywhere. In their ceaseless search for new ways to improve themselves, their neighbors, their community and the nation, the modernizers had to overpower the resistance of the traditionalists. Their success was never complete, though it was enough to establish values, institutions, and a way of life that to this day dominate Illinois.

The development of a modern lifestyle was not, of course, confined to Illinois, nor did the inspiration for it originate here. Everywhere in America and Western Europe some people were adopting modernity in the early nineteenth century. Specific events occurred in Illinois that exemplified modernization, but before we look at them we must examine the values and psychological motivations modernizers in Illinois shared with their contemporaries elsewhere in America.

The genius of the modernizers combined four interrelated, deeply held values: faith in reason, a drive for middle-class status, equal rights, and a sense of mission to transform the world in their image.

Modernizers replaced fatalism with rationality. They repudiated superstitions, folk remedies, waste, predestination, and quiet submission to fate. Reason, analysis, logical decision making were their guides, education their remedy, efficiency their ideal. Old-fashioned ways of doing things were automatically suspect, unless they could be tested and proven efficient. Science and technology could be applied with good effect in every endeavor, whether farming, business, or even child rearing. Modernizers were future oriented, and every sign of progress enhanced their confidence and propelled them forward. Obstacles to personal or social improvement, no matter how customary, were evils that deserved destruction. Gambling, speculation, drunkenness, narcotics, fighting, and wasting time were vices because they slowed the upward climb of mankind. The dozen colleges established in the thinly settled, poverty-stricken state by 1840 testified to the enormous effort modernizers devoted to the goal of bringing culture, science, and learn-ing to the frontier.

Upward mobility toward middle-class status for themselves and their children was the ambition of modernizers. Brain power was more efficient than brute force and gave more play to the creative power of reason. The more education an occupation required, the higher its status. White-collar work was especially favored because the businessman, professional, teacher, or clerk relied primarily on his intellectual talents. Skilled blue-collar occupations occupied a spectrum from traditional to modern, and were evaluated accordingly by the modernizers. At one ex-treme was the old-fashioned craftsman who followed by rote the techniques he had learned as an apprentice. This was honest labor, but it lacked an element of progress, making it unsuitable for the children of the modernizers. Much more prestigious was the restless searcher who tinkered, experimented, and invented. Henry Ford and Thomas Edison were later embodiments of this ideal; Cyrus McCormick, John Deere, and John Manney were the inventors of agricultural implements who represented the nineteenth-century engineering spirit in Illinois. Agriculture could be a high-status modern occupation, too, if the farmer read the *Prairie Farmer,* looked over new techniques at the county fair, bought the latest equipment, experimented with more efficient breeds and seeds, and produced for the market rather than quitting when he had enough food for his family. Of course, planting by the signs of the zodiac and letting animals stray were evidence of traditional farm practices that the modernizers wanted to eliminate.

The modern ideal also had contempt for the idle rich who frit-tered away their money on useless luxuries and pampered living. Many modernizers became rich, but few retired from active management of their business affairs. A handful of their off-spring did become playboys, or marry into titled European fami-lies and devote themselves to high-society fun. They were roundly condemned for squandering a golden opportunity to use their wealth for the betterment of society by enlarging factories or endowing colleges, hospitals, and libraries.

Equal rights for all men was a corollary of the universalism inherent in the modern world view. However difficult it was to achieve in practice, it shaped the modernizers' approach to law, government, and religion. The source of equal rights was more than just American republican opposition to aristocracy, for the traditionalists also shared that ideal. Rather, to the modernizers, equal rights meant that individual rewards or punishments ought to be based entirely on individual achievement or guilt, and not on favoritism or prejudice. Every man should have an equal chance to develop his talents to the fullest, to get ahead in society; as Lincoln put it, "an open field and a fair chance for your industry, enterprise and intelligence." Nepotism, inside deals, payoffs, logrolling, and prejudice were species of corruption, and ought to be eliminated in favor of equal justice under the law. The government must be strictly impartial. Men must be honest and reliable in all their dealings, not just with their friends and relatives. If men were trustworthy, if a person could make a business arrangement with a stranger without expecting to be cheated, then the economy could be developed more rapidly and everyone would be better off. Equal rights could also be applied to questions of sex and race, with the goal of eradicating male supremacy and slavery.

Unlike the short-lived utopian communities of Mormons and Icarians at Nauvoo, Swedish communists at Bishop Hill, or the Fourierists in Sangamon County, the modernizers did not withdraw from society to practice their beliefs quietly. Instead they were infused with a mission that would not end until all mankind became modern—with the idealistic hope that war, poverty, suffering, and injustice would some day be historical curiosities. Voluntary organizations, such as churches, political parties, reform clubs, study circles, missionary associations, and benevolent societies, made effective instruments for this purpose. Realizing that specialization and the systematic application of expert skills promoted progress, the modernizers introduced new modes of organization to the frontier, such as corporations, banks, colleges, railroads, and insurance companies. By concentrating talent, energy, and money on particular projects, and enlisting like-minded men and women in their causes, the modernizers created institutions that could accelerate the upward spiral of economic growth and cultural betterment.

The values of the modernizers can be traced to the ideas of the

Enlightenment, and to the philosopher-statesmen who fashioned a modern form of government for the new nation—Franklin, Adams, Jefferson, Hamilton, and Madison. Two of the most powerful early governors were associates and avid disciples of Presidents Jefferson and Madison. Yet it was one thing for a few men to write constitutions, and quite another for hundreds of thousands of persons in an economically and culturally undeveloped country to create a society that exemplified modern ideals in everyday life.

In transforming society the modernizers began with their own families. With a surer sense of control over their destiny, they limited family size through contraception (withdrawal, usually) and abstinence. Smaller families meant fewer cousins, uncles, and in-laws who could provide financial, political, or emotional support. So the nuclear family turned inward, emphasizing the intimate bonds among a husband, wife, and children. As for their relations with the outside world, they relied upon their modern skills and virtues, developing thereby an individualistic philosophy based on merit that contrasted with the traditionalist trust in kinship, patronage, and luck.

Modernizers seeking to transform humankind started with their own children. They rejected the traditionalist practices of letting children run wild, hitting them when they were a nuisance, and ignoring them otherwise. The modernizers anguished over child rearing—they read manuals and magazine articles, listened to sermons, exchanged advice, and devoted their energy and money to the best care for their children. The basic goal was to enable each child, equally, to develop his or her talents to the fullest. This required the inculcation of self-discipline, reliability, high moral standards, a maximum of schooling, and plenty of exercise, nourishing food and honest labor. Modernizers introduced regular chores into children's lives. The preferred mode of discipline was the expression of love and affection when children were good, coupled with the threat of withdrawing love when they misbehaved. Physical punishment was moderate and was applied for the child's benefit, not to express parental anger. Willy-nilly the children of the traditionalists resembled their parents; thanks to deliberate, rational effort and constant attention, the children of the modernizers surpassed their parents in developing modern personalities.[2] The children wanted to behave, follow schedules, be well-groomed, attend church and school, and become reliable, attentive, hard-working, and successful. Their parents gave them freedom because they had learned to use it properly.

Cleanliness was a major goal of the modernizing women. Women forced their menfolk to stop spitting tobacco juice and made the children bathe, wear socks and underwear, and brush their teeth. They kept stray animals out of the house and demanded privies, washbasins, bathtubs, and window screens. Although the germ theory of disease was not understood until the end of the nineteenth century, the modernizers recognized cleanliness as next to godliness. Not only did the modernizers escape body odor and hair lice, they probably had a lower incidence of colds, infections, and contagious diseases—or at least a better record than the traditionalists, who believed a person who took a bath between Christmas and New Year's would stay clean all year. By midcentury modernizers were agitating for civic hygiene—dog licenses and animal pounds to keep stray dogs, geese, and hogs from invading their premises, for example, and sanitary drinking fountains for the town square. The women repudiated folk remedies and other superstitions, demanding quality medical care from trained physicians. Whenever possible, they boycotted midwives.

The modernist commitment to equality and universalism led to a rejection of traditional male supremacy. A few brave feminists dreamed of androgyny—a society where there would be no male or female sex roles. The Shakers back East actually achieved that goal, but at the cost of enforced celibacy. The nineteenth-century modernizers instead developed the idea that the sexes could be equal if men and women each dominated separate but equally important spheres of responsibility. Men, being physically stronger and, seemingly, more aggressive,

2. Twentieth-century working-class ethnic parents often tried to make their children *unlike* themselves by using strict discipline to inculcate modern traits that they hoped would lead to middle-class status. Catholic and Lutheran parochial schools, where stern discipline was the rule, were thus popular vehicles of upward mobility for Irish, German, Polish, Italian, and even some black children.

would dominate production—specifically all employment out-side the home. Women, seen as more nutritive, aesthetic, and religious, would dominate everything within the home, includ-ing consumption, child rearing, and moral training. Men could help some around the house, but cooking, clothing, and caring for children were the wife's responsibility. Farm wives were not to work in the field, or worry about horses, cattle, hogs, or ma-chinery. Some gardening, milking, and egg-gathering was allo-cated to the women both on the farm and in villages.

The division of labor greatly enhanced the power of the house-wives. Men no longer ordered them around, and they were freed of the heavy outdoor farmwork that traditionalist women still performed. Control over spending meant that the interior of the house could be decorated attractively, and that laborsaving household appliances would be purchased when they became available. Sewing machines, stoves (rather than fireplaces), irons, upholstered furniture, carpets, even pianos began to pro-liferate, with indoor plumbing, washing machines, and refriger-ators in the future. Efficiency was as important to the housewife as it was to the breadwinner. Storekeepers responded to the woman's new role as chief shopper by sprucing up their empo-riums, adding linen sheets, ready-made clothes, corsets, and millinery to their stock, installing glass-front display cabinets, sweeping out the sawdust, and removing the spittoon. Modern merchandisers such as Potter Palmer and Marshall Field trans-formed State Street in Chicago from the wholesale to the retail trade, appealing to middle-class women from the city and down-state with dazzling window displays, fixed prices, and gentle-manly clerks and floor walkers trained to "give the lady what she wants."

Women increasingly captured morality for their sphere. A feminized, romantic religion, with heavy emphasis on Sunday Schools and women's auxiliaries, came to dominate the middle-class Methodist, Presbyterian, Congregational, and Episcopalian churches. More practically, women demanded "Victorian" sex-ual standards from their men. Taking control of their bodies, they cut back on the frequency of intercourse; many asked for separate bedrooms. Bawdy humor or even casual reference to bodily functions was banned from polite company. Jacksonville ordered stud horses out of the city limits. The traditional double standard gave way to a stern single standard of morality: no sexual activity before or outside of marriage, and little within. Little boys were taught that masturbation would turn them insane (or at least cause pimples), and prostitution became a *bête noire*. An Alton editor in 1858 commented, "Our Peoria neighbors seem very determined that no house of ill fame shall long exist in that city. Every few months they arouse themselves by demolishing one or more, without leave or license, law or officer." In Cairo, where prostitution, gambling, and liquor were major industries, the middle class was outraged at "the insults of these brazen harlots, who parade the streets daily and nightly." Smaller towns successfully eliminated the brothel, or at least made it so disreputable that middle-class men rarely visited.

Older unmarried daughters found life awkward in rural Illinois. Besides chores, there was little to do in the home except sew a trousseau or prepare for gentlemen callers. The best employment they could get was schoolteaching, and even that required demonstrating to skeptical traditionalists that they could discipline unruly adolescent boys. They won their point, and by the Civil War had forced out most of the male teachers by undercutting the pay scale. Few other jobs were available for middle-class young women before the emergence of office work in the early twentieth century. The otherwise conservative *State Register* in Springfield, arguing in 1864 that the wartime manpower shortage "offers an opportunity to make a radical change of our notions of female labor," made the drastic suggestion that "the introduction of female clerks into stores where light groceries, fancy goods, ladies' shoes, etc., are sold, would have a good influence upon the public manners." Millinery and dressmaker shops and music teaching offered a little opportunity in the towns. A few widows ran boardinghouses. Service and laundry work and midwifery were the province of the poorest working-class women. Nursing as a profession came later. The woman who exercised any power in government, commerce, finance, industry, or the professions was an extreme rarity. In Peoria, Mrs. Lydia Bradley was a director of the largest bank after its founder, her husband, died. In Bloomington a woman became school superintendent in 1874, over the protests of men who thought business rather than teaching experience was more important in a post that controlled a $60,000 annual budget. Bloomington was unusual in that all of the grammar school principals were women, though the more prestigious high school principal was a man.

Nearly all modernizing women accepted, indeed, demanded the two-sphere system. After all, it gave them less work, more power, a deeper emotional life with husband and children, and open-ended freedom to enjoy either leisure or outside activity. Surplus energy available after home duties were fulfilled could be absorbed by voluntary societies. Beginning with the Ladies Education Society, which began helping poor girls become teachers in Jacksonville in 1833 (it was America's first woman's club), the number and range of outlets grew rapidly. Women predominated in temperance and antislavery societies. In little Prairie City near Peoria, the women protested the single tavern: "We regret exceedingly the necessity of our seeming in any way to interfere with the management of our village, but our hearts have been pained by the results of the liquor traffic to the unfortunate victims of intemperance and their defenseless families." The tavern lost its license. In a dozen towns where in 1854 the law moved slower, however, women brandishing hatchets, shovels, and rolling pins destroyed whiskey barrels and saloon furnishings.

The women demanded, and slowly won, equal access to collegiate education, favorable widow's property laws, and child custody rights. They resented discrimination when their own sphere was at stake. "Are we simply dolls? Puppets in pantomime?" raged an indignant woman who noticed in 1860 that no women were judges at the state fair. "We are co-equal in judgment with the masculine gender in all that pertains to domestic affars." If her husband endorsed the fair's policy, she added, "he would go with holes in his stockings for the next six months."

Voting, however, was considered squarely in the male sphere before the Civil War. Feminists who honed their organizational skills by massive fundraising campaigns for medical supplies during the war organized the suffrage movement in the late

1860s. They argued that prostitution, drunkenness, and poverty could only be destroyed if women—with their superior moral intuition and desire to protect the home—had some political power. Responding to the petition of feminists for "a more perfect freedom and equality" the delegates to the 1870 state constitutional convention decided to submit the equal suffrage question to the male electorate. To their surprise, however, housewives began voicing strong opposition. A petition from Peoria signed by 1,300 women protested: "That woman's sphere is distinct from man's, and is well defined; and that, as going to the polls forms no part of it, we will strenuously oppose this movement as an invasion of our right not to do man's work." Denouncing the suffragists for "grasping after duties, powers and privileges that naturally belong to the stronger sex," the antis feared that blurring the roles of men and women would cost them the gains recently achieved by modernizing wives. The convention then reversed its approval of woman suffrage. Only in 1913, when a majority of Illinois women had come to accept the proposition that wives had to protect their home sphere by use of the ballot, did men give them the vote.

Enthusiastic volunteer work was essential to the momentum of voluntary reform organizations the modernizers developed. Local, even statewide, groups formed from the 1830s onward to press for better education, abolition of slavery, foreign missions, temperance, cultural enlightenment, and every good civic purpose the reformers could imagine. The energy devoted to these causes was phenomenal. A Congregational minister reported to his diary in 1842 that he had "attended the first meeting for mutual improvement at Knoxville; also the other association . . . but was compelled to tear myself away, as my house and family needed my attention, for it is very cold and our house has neither doors nor floors." It was Christmas Eve.

Mass education, modernizers believed, was the ultimate long-term panacea for eradicating ignorance, superstition, and traditionalism, and for ushering in an era of self-perpetuating social and economic modernization. Private schools sprang up, supported by parents' tuition. Although the state had a vast reserve of wealth earmarked for school support in the form of one township in every thirty-six, public education began very

slowly. A long series of state laws permitting the use of tax revenues for schools was ineffective. Only in 1855, when the modernizers had control of the state legislature, did legislation pass
compelling public schools to be formed. The resistance of traditionalists to paying taxes for the benefit of others' children was
intense, and was overcome only by promising a double share of
state revenues for the southern counties. Progress was rapid
after that. Springfield set up a public school system in 1856,
soon adding a separate school for black children. Most teachers
were local youth with no more than eight years of schooling
themselves. To overcome this deficiency the larger cities established high schools, and beginning with Peoria in 1853,
teacher's colleges were established at Bloomington, Carbondale, Peoria, and Chicago. The untrained rural teachers
began attending country institutes where standard pedagogical
techniques were discussed. Soon the more progressive school
districts were hiring only high school graduates. By the early
twentieth century modernizers were able to convince traditionalistic skeptics that investment in education was worthwhile.

The modernizers worked to transform Illinois from subsistence agriculture and barter to a market economy, with cash
crops, good transportation, expansive commerce, new manufacturing, and a supportive banking system. In settling the land
they ignored the river bottoms and hills of southern Illinois
where subsistence was easy but markets were hard to reach. Instead they boldly moved into the treeless prairies where large
wheat and corn crops could be raised. They sought out the latest
agricultural improvements, such as John Deere's plow and
Cyrus McCormick's harvester. County fairs and magazines like
Prairie Farmer brought them the newest and most efficient
techniques for handling crops, animals, and farm supplies. They
experimented with a new crop, sorghum, and new breeds of
cattle, horses, and sheep. The fabulous fertility of the prairie
soil meant limitless prosperity as soon as transportation to distant markets became possible.

In the 1830s a mania for instant modernization of the economy excited every politician and entrepreneur in the state. The
construction of a canal that would eventually link Lake Michigan with the Illinois and Mississippi rivers drew speculators

to the marshes of Chicago, where swampy lots were suddenly traded for tens of thousands of dollars. Real estate everywhere was in heavy demand, as new banks printed money freely for distribution to speculators who quickly passed it to the federal land office. After elaborate logrolling in the legislature, the state committed its credit to a multimillion dollar system of canals and railroads that was supposed to prosper by carrying farm produce to distant markets.

The boom collapsed totally. In Washington, President Andrew Jackson ordered land offices to accept only gold and silver. This action touched off a financial panic, ruined the banks in Illinois, bankrupted every Chicago real estate operator, and drastically reduced the sales of farmland. The canal from Chicago to the Illinois River was delayed, not to open until 1848. Construction on the great network of railroads and canals began everywhere simultaneously but was never finished. The state was left with useless embankments and muddy ditches going nowhere, and with a crushing debt that took decades to repay.

Recriminations over the failure of premature modernization polarized politics along modern-versus-traditional lines. The modernizers blamed the disaster on inept planning by patronage-hungry politicians. Private enterprise would have done the job right, they claimed. The great majority of businessmen, financiers, and entrepreneurs joined together to form a new party, the Whigs. Henry Clay's policies—federal encouragement of internal improvements, a strong national banking system, and tariff protection for emerging industry—became their formula for rapid economic modernization. Jacksonian Democrats' attacks on banks, paper money, and transportation improvements would delay the emergence of a national market economy, they feared. The Whigs proudly claimed the allegiance of "a large proportion of the mercantile class—the shifting, bustling, speculating class." A Jacksonville correspondent said he was unable to provide a list of Democratic businessmen, for "all of our solvent businessmen are opposed to the [Democratic] Administration."

The Democrats raised the banner of traditionalism. Paper money, banks, wild-eyed internal improvement schemes were frauds on the honest subsistence farmer. Tariffs would raise prices only for the benefit of the rich. Government promotion of modernity—whether economic, social, or cultural—was wrong-headed. Although some wealthy landowners and lawyers belonged to the Democratic party, it became increasingly the defensive vehicle of the subsistence farmer and the unskilled laborer, and it never flagged in its attacks on the men of wealth and ambition who formed the opposition. A Democratic farmer in Clay County captured the spirit exactly when he denounced the Whiggish "rage to be genteel, extravagant and refined, [which] has raised every upstart in this country above the decree of his Maker, that man shall gain his bread by the sweat of his brow."

Recent voting studies underscore the polarization that occured along class lines. In Greene County in the 1840s, for example, 67 percent of the poorest fourth of the population voted Democratic, 63 percent of the middle half, and only 46 percent of the richest fourth. Farmers were 64 percent Democratic, while non-farmers were 62 percent Whig. Thus, of the merchants, clergymen, and physicians, forty-nine were Whigs and only twenty-two Democrats. The lawyers, however, divided five to five, and the Democratic and Whig candidates for office both were more than twice as rich as their respective rank and file. As we shall see later in this chapter, economic indicators like wealth and occupation are only part of the story—the crucial factor of the religious basis of modernization and therefore of party identification must also be considered.

By 1840 nearly every man in Illinois had chosen sides in the fierce political contests that enraged, enthralled, and entertained the citizenry every two years. The Democrats always had the potential advantage, for traditionalist farmers, Irishmen, and Germans outnumbered the modernizers until the mid-1850s. To turn this advantage into electoral victories, the Democrats structured their party like an army, with strict discipline—that is, intense party loyalty—inculcated into the ranks. As one Whig, former Gov. Joseph Duncan, explained, "The rank and file are forced to ratify every bargain made by their leaders, however repugnant . . . for most men would sacrifice their country, and compromise their honor, or their principles, sooner than encounter the sneers, much less the obloquy and scorn of a party, after having firmly enlisted under its banner." Or as an opposition newspaper put it, the Democrats must "be led up to the polls by a twine through the gristle of the proboscis." To be sure, the typical Democrat did not see it this way. He rejoiced in the strength created by unity. The hierarchical structure of his party and the deep sense of loyalty accorded well with his psychology of traditionalism. Division and confusion were spared the Democrats, who were always sure of what to believe, of whom to vote for. They responded enthusiastically, turning out for rallies, picnics, speechfests and, most important, turning out at the polls. Between 1838 and 1848, 62 percent of the Democrats living in Greene County voted in at least six of eight elections, a far higher proportion than today.

An organized party, like an army, explained Duncan, "must have captains, subalterns, and drill masters, who . . . expect to be rewarded for their services, when successful, out of the spoils." The Democrats could be generous, for they controlled the bulk of the local, county, state, and federal jobs in Illinois—many of them extremely lucrative—and gave them all out on the basis of service. "Thus stimulated by ambition and self-interest," fumed the cynical ex-governor, the politicians "meet in secret, without individual responsibility . . . and then devise means for destroying their opponents, and for deceiving and managing the people. They are the inquisitorial judges of the merits and demerits of all persons in office, and recommend rewards or punishments, not according to services rendered or to be rendered to the country, but to the party." Stephen Douglas, undisputed master of the Democratic party in Illinois, followed the same policy: "I shall act on the rule of giving the offices to those who fight the battles." He saw his party threatened by demoralization when the rewards went to drones instead of faithful workers. "Our first duty is to the cause," he wrote his closest ally, "the fate of individual politicians is of minor importance."

To ensure strict loyalty, regular conventions nominated the party candidates; dissenters faced punishment; ticket-splitting was strongly discouraged. Hard-working local politicians enlisted every available man and marched him to the polls. An effective network of well-edited weekly newspapers provided excellent communications within the party, knitting the state together and linking it with the national leadership in Washington. Jammed with lists of meetings, reprints of speeches, tidbits of gossip on the comings and goings of minor candidates, and always explicit on the ideas, arguments, promises, and programs of the party, the newspapers served the interested citizen well. The opposition always was bested in its pages—its leaders corrupt, its voters confused, its ideas foolish, its rallies failures. Thus the leading Democratic paper "reported" a Lincoln rally in 1860: Some "boys and little girls, some men and a few inquisitive old women came together. . . . The glee club struck up a most unmusical air, at which the sleepers yawned and the thin audience wriggled." The famous eastern orator was a carpetbagger; his eloquence all froth and foam, his glamor merely due to "remarkable teeth and moustache." Illinois politics could be fun sometimes!

More often it was deadly serious, hard work. Caucuses in the legislature kept the solons in line for party votes, while lucrative offices like postmaster or marshal whetted the ambition of aspiring workers. To co-ordinate such an elaborate organization the Democrats needed some modern men, preferably lawyers or wealthy farmers who could spare the time. While most of this class were Whigs, enough were Democrats to serve the purpose. The result was that the Democratic leadership had the same profile in terms of wealth, education, and occupation as the Whigs, despite the sharp difference between the respective rank and files.

The Whig party had little difficulty finding eminent candidates and sharp-witted editors. Its problem was the bias among its less traditional membership against blind loyalty. In 1835 Whig legislators denounced the convention system as "anti-republican," and it took strenuous efforts by Lincoln and other professional politicians to establish this basic form of party discipline. In 1840 the Whigs developed enthusiasm by an appeal to fraternity instead of loyalty. Massive rallies, long parades, exuberant speeches, and lavish barbecues brought the Whigs together, arm in arm, banker with farmer, merchant with laborer, in a display of uncoerced solidarity that amazed the Democrats. They hurrahed for "Tippicanoe and Tyler too" around log cabins that symbolized their faith that any poor boy could rise in America, even to president. Thereafter the Whigs kept together by attacking the malevolent machine the Democrats had created. The antipartyism among modernists, however, prevented the formation of deep partisan loyalties. The professional leaders, most notably Lincoln, realized in 1852 that the Whig ticket would never carry the state or nation again. They dropped politics for more promising commercial or professional pursuits.

Thus far we have characterized the psychology of the modernizers, but we have not described who they were, nor explained why they became modernizers. The first task is a little easier. In the nineteenth century the Yankees were almost synonymous with modernizers. These migrants from New England (or intermediate points in New York, Ohio, etc.) brought with them a modernized outlook developed in the advanced society back East. They concentrated in northern Illinois, where the prairie soil was suited only for commercial agriculture and where waterfalls on the Rock and Fox rivers promised an opportunity to build manufacturing towns. Famous for their ambition, hard work, and shrewd bargains, the Yankees soon prospered greatly. In 1870, Yankee farmers were worth 50 percent more than other farmers. Nearly all the great industrial and financial entrepreneurs of nineteenth-century Illinois were Yankees—Deere, Swift, Ogden, Field, Armour, etc.[3]

The Yankees of Winnebago County beamed when an eastern reporter wrote them up for a leading New York newspaper:

> Like their fathers at Plymouth Rock, they will have meeting houses and common schools. . . . They are generally sober, industrious, enterprising and moral. A large majority of them would vote for the Maine Liquor Law [i.e., prohibition]. They read the Bible on Sunday and the New York Tribune and *Uncle Tom's Cabin* all the rest of the week.

A perceptive governor agreed that Yankees stood out in liberal contributions for public benefit. "Is a schoolhouse, a bridge, or

---

3. The one striking exception was Cyrus McCormick, the reaper magnate, who came from Virginia. Apart from manufacturing, however, he was an intensely traditional opponent of religious and political reform. His associates and high-level employees were Republicans, as were his heirs, who married Yankees.

a church to be built, a road to be made, a school or minister to be maintained, or taxes to be paid? . . . The northern man is never found wanting."

Modernizers appeared in other groups, though not as frequently or as prominently as among Yankees. Swedish and British immigrants also brought modern outlooks with them to northern Illinois, and they quickly established themselves as prosperous farmers, craftsmen, foremen, engineers, and clerks. The Swedes were especially active in the temperance crusade.

Farmers from the middle states who came to central Illinois fell somewhere in the middle of the modern-traditional continuum. As early as 1812 a visitor found that settlers from New Jersey and Pennsylvania,

> particularly of the Scotch and Irish descent, are very ready to unite in promoting the establishment of schools and in supporting the gospel, whilst those of German extraction, together with emigrants from Maryland, Virginia and Kentucky, are too frequently regardless of both, and too often cherish that high-toned and licentious spirit which will suffer neither contradiction nor opposition and which is equally inconsistent with civil and religious order.

Distrustful of new ways, yet willing enough to make an extra dollar, they rarely adopted technological innovations until they were thoroughly convinced, by actual observation, that they more than paid their way. Wedded to agriculture, they avoided the city and thought it wasteful to spend a nickle more than necessary on education. Their economic status was average, with few men of wealth.

The German immigrants who made Illinois the center of German-American culture fell on the moderately traditional part of the spectrum. They were literate, hard-working, and had money, but they also nurtured strong extended families, preferred farming as a way of life, and devoutly practiced either highly liturgical Roman Catholicism or extremely scholastic Lutheranism. They opposed reform, especially temperance, and distrusted banks and Yankee-dominated public schools. Politically they favored the Democratic party. Economically they were average in 1870. Geographically they dispersed in rural areas and cities on a line from Saint Louis to Springfield to

Chicago. By the late nineteenth century, Germans were the largest element in both Saint Louis and Chicago. Germans who grew restless with their tight-knit ethnic communities frequently converted to Methodism, abandoned use of their mother tongue, and assimilated into the Yankee community. Far fewer in number, though far more attention-grabbing, were the thoroughly modernized German political refugees, the forty-eighters. They were militant reformers, opponents of slavery and clericalism, and they rapidly found success in politics, journalism, and business.

The Irish Catholics who fled famine and British repression poured into Illinois in the 1840s and 1850s to work on canal or railroad construction crews. They concentrated in the cities, particularly Chicago, where the men were low-paid day laborers and the women worked as servants or laundresses. Crime, fighting, drunkenness, broken homes, and abject poverty were endemic in their shanty towns for decades. From the 1850s to the 1870s, half the paupers in the Cook County almshouse were Irish. What little wealth the community accumulated went toward building churches, convents, and parochial schools. By isolating themselves from the outer world, especially from the cultural influence of the modernizing Yankees who dominated the public schools and the economy, the Irish slowed their rate of upward occupational mobility to a crawl, yet also developed a sense of group loyalty that proved politically irresistible.

Already in the 1850s, the Irish had tightly embraced the Democratic party. Their saloons became precinct headquarters, and their reward was patronage. By the mid-1850s a fifth of the elected or appointed government officials in Chicago were Irish. Bitterly opposed to reform, especially abolitionism, the Irish appeared to the modernizers as the most serious challenge to the success of good government. The Whigs attempted to limit the speed with which the Irish could become citizens, or at least to curb their penchant for multiple voting and violence at the polls. After the Whigs collapsed, a secret political movement—dubbed the Know-Knothings—mobilized middle-class fear of the Irish, and for a while controlled Chicago. Nativism proved a dilemma for the Republicans, who needed the votes of ex-Know-Nothings in 1856 and 1860, yet also needed some German support. By focusing attention on the evils of the slavocracy of the South, the Republicans finally resolved the dilemma, though they never captured more than a small fraction of the Irish vote.

Southerners continued to arrive in Illinois, especially Egypt, the southern third. The great majority remained subsistence farmers through the Civil War era; their wealth was about half the state average, and they steadfastly rejected reform or innovation of any sort. An exasperated reaper salesman sputtered at them in 1856:

> If the *coon dog* and *butcher knife* tribe can ever be rooted out or killed off who occupy the best land along the [Illinois] Central we might hope to do something with Reapers and wheat drills, improved plows, etc., in that region. . . . The present population are pretty smart raising castor beans and chickens but that is all they can do.

Illinois did attract some ambitious southerners who deliberately copied the Yankee model. As Lincoln's law partner confided to a friend, "I am a southerner—born on southern soil—reared by southern parents, but I have always turned New-Englandwards for my ideas—my sentiments—my education." On the other hand, the state's outstanding politicians were southerners, notably Kentuckians like Lincoln. Stephen Douglas was a Vermonter, but he deliberately ridiculed Yankees, adopted southern ways, married a southern wife, and through her came into control of a large plantation stocked with slaves. His second wife was a Roman Catholic. The aura of strong personal leadership cultivated by the southerners was one heritage of traditionalism that stood them well in politics.

Abraham Lincoln was the outstanding exemplar of the self-made modern man. Born to illiterate parents (his father forgot how to sign his name) who fled from one adversity to a worse one, Lincoln scrambled desperately for learning as an escape from the lazy life of a backwoods wrestler, dirt farmer, and teller of dirty stories that he seemed destined for. He refused to join the highly traditionalistic Baptist church and early repudiated the Democratic faith of his kinfolk. Instead he became an avid follower of Henry Clay, and an advocate of banks, tariffs, railroads, and economic modernization. He was a teetotaler—although he never joined any church—and he avoided gambling, hunting, and brawling. Lincoln became a lawyer, an easy task for a good reader, and between his work for corporations rode the circuit through central Illinois. His forte was bridging the gap between the arcane forms of the common law and the needs of simple, traditionalistic folk. Politically, however, his support came from men of wealth and ambition. Lincoln fervently held that the upward mobility so highly prized by modernizers was an ideal—and a reality—that was worth fighting for. He sketched the career of the "prudent, penniless beginner"—such as he had been—who labors for wages, saves and borrows to buy land and tools, and emerges prosperous enough to hire others. If anyone failed to rise, Lincoln added, it was because of laziness, folly, or "singular misfortune," and most decidedly not the fault of "the just and generous and prosperous system, which opens the way for all—gives hope to all, and energy, and progress, and improvement of condition to all." To be sure, Lincoln did not promise equality of condition to all, though rural Illinois before the Civil War was in fact characterized by equality. Everyone was poor. A check of all 3,000 families in three typical counties [4] of central Illinois in 1850, for example, shows only 136 farmers worth more than $2,500 in land, property, and securities, along with only 27 nonfarmers. The richest farmer reported $15,000, the richest lawyer $5,000. The wealthiest nonfarmer was a merchant worth $50,000, and the second was worth only $10,000. After the war, however, urbanization and the rise in land prices caused the spread between rich and poor to grow dramatically.

Everyone in Illinois recognized the difference between modernizers and traditionalists—despite the fact that nobody used those words. Each group thought the other peculiar. Fast-talking Yankee peddlers were distrusted—one county even set a prohibitive $50 per quarter license for clock peddlers. A Yankee woman was amused by the drinking, horse trading, and quaint slow drawl of the southerners. She talked with one who " 'allows it's a right smart thing to be able to read when you

---

4. DeWitt, Cumberland, and Shelby counties. Slightly more than half reported no wealth, apart from clothes and tools. The mean wealth was only $1,000.

want to,' but he don't 'calculate' that books and the sciences will do as much good for a man in these matters as a handy use of the rifle." As for teaching, she probed, "that's the one thing he allows the Yankees are just fit for . . . they are a 'power smarter' at that than the Western boys. But they can't hold a rifle nor ride a wolf hunt with 'em; and he reckons, after all, these are the great tests of merit."

The emergence of a Yankee-dominated, more urban, modern northern Illinois polarized the state along north-south lines, with the central third holding the balance of power in elections. Any reform issue would sweep the north, be buried in Egypt, and be decided by the center. Thus statewide referenda on banking (1851), prohibition (1855), and the exclusion of Negroes (1848) showed strong sectional alignments. In 1860, for example, Lincoln won 70 percent of the vote in the north, and a mere 20 percent down in Egypt. On the eve of the Civil War the *Chicago Tribune* found that the deadly hostility of national politics was mirrored in Illinois: "It breaks out upon all possible occasions—in the personal intercourse of the [legislators], in their speeches touching matters in which national politics are not concerned, in their views of state policy, of education and of internal improvements."

Economic development was far more rapid in the north, while the central region was slow to catch up, and Egypt lagged far behind. Modernizers argued that the superb soil of the central region "with a little Yankee enterprise would soon become a beautiful country. But in consequence of the idle habits of the inhabitants [of Mason and Tazewell counties] it is far behind the northern portion of Illinois, although having many natural advantages over it." After the Civil War wealthy absentee landlords set about developing the central area by insisting that their tenants give up traditional practices to adopt the best equipment and most modern farming practices. Railroad corporations and coal mining magnates began tapping the natural resources of Egypt, giving that area an almost colonial economy.

The educational differential between more modern and more traditional areas of the state persisted well into the twentieth century. In 1883, the northern part of the state provided its children with a third more days of schooling than Egypt. De

Kalb County (where Northern Illinois University would later be established) gave its children 69 percent more class days than Jackson County, where Southern Illinois University had operated for a decade. Furthermore, De Kalb had several fine high schools and Jackson none. Those few youth in Egypt who did obtain higher education came overwhelmingly from the small modern sector. Among students at Southern Illinois in 1883 the offspring of physicians, lawyers, and merchants outnumbered the sons and daughters of laborers, mechanics, carpenters, and blacksmiths by a ratio of five to one.

Modernization is addictive. Once a group is exposed to it, its members cannot turn back—or at least rarely and reluctantly do so. Instead they demand more of themselves and their children: more and more skill, self-discipline, education, innovation, and achievement. This pattern has been called the revolution of rising expectations, and it struck Illinois hard in the midnineteenth century. True, some groups held back, and the net progress of the state toward modernity was set back for a while when new, highly traditional elements like the Irish arrived. Eventually the Irish too discovered the upward escalator of modernization, until by the late twentieth century the Irish Catholics were wealthier and better educated, on the whole, than even the Yankees. Old people sometimes had a hard time keeping up with progress. They waxed nostalgic, as the numerous "old settlers" meetings in the late nineteenth century attested: "Singer's Sewing Machine that *never* sings is no compensation for the loss of the blue eyed girls that sewed and sang in the old homesteads. Wooden harvesters do not sing harvest songs; iron mowers do not drink from cold springs." The young ladies of earlier days, recalled a pioneer,

> didn't wear silks and ruffles, nor fritz and bang their hair; they were content with linsey-woolsey dresses made by their own hands. The loom was their piano, and the spinning wheel their organ. . . .
> They sought the washtub and broomhandle for exercise. Girls of the present day would almost faint at the sight of such things.

Religion played a crucial role in determining whether a person would incline more toward the modern or traditional pole. In the nineteenth century religion was a much more powerful influence than it is today, largely because it was a new experience to most people. Very few Americans were church members in 1800; a hundred years later the majority were. Old-stock settlers became religious when revivals stirred a profound sense of guilt, followed by a conversion experience. Immigrants from Germany and Ireland and Scandinavia established their identity in this strange new land by enthusiastic participation in Catholic or Lutheran activities, in striking contrast to their apathy or hostility toward the established churches in their motherland.

Some denominations, notably the Roman Catholics, German Lutherans, and southern-dominated Baptists, were intensely inwardly directed. Members avoided outsiders, married within the fold, paid careful attention to orthodox beliefs and (as did Catholics and Lutherans), followed closely the leadership of their pastors. Each believed theirs was the only true church, which reinforced their particularism, and made them very hostile to any interference by the government in the realm of morality. Thus, their religion was strongly traditional. They heatedly opposed reformers—usually Yankees—who advocated prohibition, abolition of slavery, women's rights, and compulsory public education. The Democratic party reflected their beliefs and won their strong loyalty. "Is this the age when virtue, religion and morals are to be forced upon us?" asked a leading Democrat. More than 90 percent of the Irish Catholics voted Democratic for a whole century—from the 1840s to the 1940s, and to this day they are mostly Democrats. German-Catholic voting was almost as heavily Democratic before 1896, when it began swinging wildly. German Lutherans were also Democrats before 1896, though Republicans did make significant inroads into their ranks. Baptists of southern origins were heavily Democratic, at least until the Civil War. In Greene County in the 1840s, for example, 75 percent of the Baptists of southern origins were Democrats, and they supported their party more regularly and enthusiastically than other Democrats.

Pulling hard for modernity were the pietistic Congregationalists, Presbyterians, Methodists, and Baptists from New England. They rejected the particularism of Calvinists and Catholics, opting instead for the universalistic belief that all men can be reached by God's grace, be converted and saved. Concern with their souls made them introspective and future-oriented. They set up missionary societies that channelled thousands of dollars annually from New England to scores of missionaries in Illinois. When the missionaries realized they were reaching few besides Yankees, they turned to education, establishing academies and colleges (notably Illinois College in Jacksonville, Knox in Galesburg, and Northwestern in Evanston). They rallied their congregations to the temperance and antislavery causes, and condemned gambling, idleness, and frivolity. In Greene County, the combination of a modern New England heritage and a modernizing religious faith produced solid Whig voting. Presbyterians and Methodists born in the Northeast were 90 percent Whig, while those with a more traditional southern background were only 70 percent Whig.

The pietistic Protestants saw the growing strength of the Catholic church as a major obstacle to the eventual modernization of Illinois. Eminent intellectuals hurled tirades against the "whore of Babylon"—Elijah Lovejoy mixed violent attacks on Catholics and slavery until he was shot defending his press from an angry mob. Jesuits, nunneries, and a tide of "corrupt" Democratic Irish Catholics animated Protestant sermons. "Why is it that the Catholics are pursued with such pertinacity, such vindictiveness, with such ruthless malevolence?" demanded a fairminded editor in 1835. "We speak kindly of the Jew, and even of the heathen; there are those who love a negro or a Cherokee even better than their own flesh and blood; but a Catholic is an abomination, for whom there is no law." It was hardly a wonder that the Catholics voted against the Yankees at every turn!

The Protestants may have united in their anti-Catholicism, but they were also highly competitive with each other. The frontier was ripe for conversion, and each denomination tried to undercut the others, whether with ridicule or learned theology, so as to reap the harvest. Within each denomination, tension emerged between the more and the less modern elements. The Presbyterians split in two in 1837, with the more traditionalistic

Scotch-Irish forming an "Old School" body, strongest in southern Illinois, as the Yankees worked through the more modern, reformist "New School." The Baptists were bitterly divided over the wisdom of reform measures, missionary societies, and education. The more traditionalistic Baptists held to predestination, while the modern faction resembled the Yankees. The Methodists' leadership headed off disruption. Their theology had a universalistic theme, and as their members prospered they paid less attention to revivals and became more interested in reform. However, the poorer, simpler, more devout Methodists were alienated by growing superficiality after the Civil War, and drifted into Holiness, Nazarene, and Pentecostal groups. The Disciples of Christ likewise split, with the more traditional faction becoming the Church of Christ. In the Episcopal Church, furious battles over the traditionalism of the high-church liturgical wing kept the membership in turmoil until after the Civil War.

In general the modern wing in each denomination inclined to the Whig-Republican fold, to reform, and to upward mobility, while the traditionalists tried to resist change in both society and politics. "There is scarcely a Protestant church member in Chicago, or a temperance man, who is not an ardent Republican," noted one newspaper in 1858. The mixing of politics and religion caught Democratic fire: "The black republican clergy in the [1856] campaign . . . turned their pulpits into political rostrums." During the Civil War, a number of local congregations were ripped apart by debates on emancipation. The minority faction was silenced, expelled, or withdrew to more congenial bodies.

Later converts to modernity lacked something of the moral absolutism and evangelical fervor typical of the Yankees. They emphasized practicality and efficiency, and their consciences less often spoiled a good business opportunity or advantageous political trade by nagging doubts about morality. Their "live and let live" attitude set a tolerant tone for the politics of central Illinois, in contrast to the more rigid standards that prevailed in Yankee or Swedish settlements in the northern tier of counties. Whereas Yankee children inclined to scholarship, the learned professions, and missionary endeavors, the other modern types favored business pursuits and saw high school and college as opportunities for practical knowledge rather than fonts of aesthetic or scientific wisdom.

To explain why some people became modernizers and others remained traditionalists is like trying to explain why some people are ambitious and others are lazy. Neither psychology nor history has a complete answer. We can speculate that when people adopted the universalistic norms of pietistic Christianity they became exposed to powerful modern influences. But this only pushes the question back one step: why did some convert and others not? The culture and historic experiences of different groups were predisposing factors. The Yankees were familiar with the effectiveness of voluntary societies in religious affairs, reform, and organized migration. The Germans, Scandinavians, and British could see the achievements of economic and political modernization in their homeland, and being denied the benefits thereof by hierarchical social structures, yearned for the combination of freedom and progress available in America. The less ambitious of their countrymen, as well as the more privileged, could and did remain home. The southerners, blacks, and Irish-Catholic groups came to Illinois to escape oppression or avert starvation. In their destitution they emphasized group solidarity, militancy, male supremacy, and distrust of strangers for self-protection. They had a low sense of efficacy in dealing with difficult ideas, complex organizations, or new modes of technology. The southerners responded by turning inward, relying heavily on family alliances. The blacks developed a sense of race pride that belied their disorganized lifestyle (largely forced upon them by intense white hostility). The Irish turned to their authoritarian church, and soon to politics. They discovered that disciplined, co-ordinated voting paid off handsomely in the whirligig of urban politics. Each group was characterized by high levels of poverty and crime, and also by disrespect for the law.

Traditionalists existed side by side with modernists in every group in Illinois; only the relative proportions differed. After the Civil War Illinois became increasingly wealthy—money was to be made in commerce, manufacturing, farming, and, especially, land speculation. The lure of money for traditionalists was as strong as for anyone—though their emphasis was probably more on reducing hardship than on giving full reign to creative abilities (the latter, of course, being a very modern attitude). The modernizers deliberately provided a model for success which any traditional youth with ambition could emulate. The schools, especially, became agencies for inculcating modern attitudes, with the promise of middle-class status and wealth for those who applied themselves. Likewise, the industrial discipline of the factory forced workers to adopt at least a few modern habits, like punctuality and acceptance of technology, for those who wanted to make good money. Every year some traditionalists came to terms with modernity, while very few modernists pursued the reverse course. Two differences remained between groups like the Yankees, who modernized first, and the latecomers. The former achieved dominance in the highest ranks of business, banking, and the professions, and still keep their hold to this day. Also the Yankees, and perhaps the Scandinavians, have always been more reform-oriented, less tolerant of corruption, even if it was economically advantageous. Thus it happened that entire groups became a little more modern every year, until the remnants of traditionalism faded away—or perhaps were transformed into an interest in music, sports, festivals, and hunting. Children began donning Hallowe'en costumes that mimicked the goblins their ancestors believed in.[5]

The gradual conversion from traditionalism to modernity should not mislead us into seeing Illinois as a land of harmony. At any one time the difference between the most and least modern elements in Illinois was wide. Conflict, particularly in the arenas of politics and religion, and later in labor-management relations, remained tense. Violence often occurred when the opposing groups were in direct physical contact, especially at election time in the cities or during strikes. Fortunately, the state was big enough to accept a certain degree of heterogeneity. How Illinois would have developed if national events had not intervened is impossible for anyone to predict. The question of what

5. The blacks were a partial exception. Cut off by de facto segregation from outlets for their ambitions, and regularly reinforced by an influx of highly traditional migrants from the deep South, their traditionalism continued very strong.

values the state would support became more than academic in 1861: Civil War broke out in America, and on a small scale in Illinois itself. The war forced men and women back upon their deepest values—values worth fighting for. The modernizers eventually won out, but as the next chapter will demonstrate, the war lasted forty years.

3

War for Modernity, 1860–1896

AMERICANS in the 1850s argued over which fundamental principles should be paramount in the nation. The intensity of involvement reached a pitch seldom attained in the United States. When men saw that no amount of argumentation could resolve the issue, they mobilized armies and shot it out in a four-year Civil War that devastated a third of the country. Victory on the battlefield was not enough to settle the issues, as a decade of "reconstruction" of national values proved. More than a century passed before national consensus was reached on one key issue, racial equality. Illinois played a leading role in defining the issues and deciding the outcome of the war and the peace settlement. While the human and material sacrifices of the state were soon recovered, the emotional impact lingered for a generation. In the end, the forces of rapid modernization triumphed and gave Illinois momentum for a century of further development.

Had the tension between modernity and traditionalism been the simple issue in the 1850s, war could have been avoided. It was not so simple. Great national leaders, Lincoln and Douglas most famously, cut through the verbiage of political rhetoric to a bedrock of values that, in the circumstances of the day, were incompatible. "Important principles may, and must, be inflexible," declared Abraham Lincoln, the man whose vision ultimately triumphed by sheer force.

Four basic values, two modern, two traditional, were central:

61

free labor and nationalism on the one hand, popular democracy and property rights on the other. On all sides in the 1850s was a general consensus in favor of white supremacy—a consensus that crumbled in the exigencies of total war and opened the path to new conflicts. To be sure, other issues from time to time attracted attention—prohibition, corruption, nativism, internal improvements, free homestead land, banking, tariffs, even polygamy. When the crisis came these issues paled into insignificance, to re-emerge only when the four basic values were settled one way or another. The political debates of the era were invariably cast in constitutional language, which meant that even appeals to traditionalism had to be phrased in modern, universalistic terms. The parties had their opportunity to clarify the issues, and the result was a reshuffling of loyalties and alignments that produced four presidential candidates in 1860, one for each principle. That contest produced a clear-cut result, the election of Lincoln, that drove the states in the deep South to secession, followed by recourse to coercion, more secession, and finally full-scale warfare.

One position, that of the Republicans, so well articulated by an otherwise obscure Illinois man that it won him the presidency, was that the free labor basis of modernity must become universal in America. The free labor doctrine meant that slavery was an evil that had to be put on the road to extinction. Until the Emancipation Proclamation, no one could say how that was to be accomplished, nor until after the war could Republicans come up with any solution to the dilemma of a large, free, black population, lacking civil rights and living in the midst of a majority that strongly adhered to white supremacy. The vision of an end to slavery included the promise that the South could be modernized. Republicans saw the South as a feudal regime, dominated by an aristocracy of slaveowners, where luxury and laziness had displaced thrift, where stagnation impeded economic growth, where ignorance and barbarism stymied cultural advancement, and where easy sexual license between master and slave girl destroyed the basis for modern family life on the part of whites and blacks both. The picture was grossly exaggerated, but it ignited a moralistic crusade to remedy the evil.

The momentum that carried the Republicans to power came

less from their dream of transforming the slave states than from their fear that slavery was a vastly powerful, sinister force that had captured the federal government and was fast extending its tentacles into the western territories, and threatened even Illinois. The Kansas-Nebraska bill of 1854 crystallized this fear. The northern part of the Louisiana Purchase, supposedly safe from slavery because of the Missouri Compromise of 1820, was now open to the menace. The miniature civil war that erupted in Kansas and the maneuvers of the Pierce and Buchanan administrations in favor of a clear minority of Kansas slaveowners proved the danger was real. More chilling was the Supreme Court's Dred Scott decision of 1857, which held that Congress had no power to keep slaves out of the territories. In his debates with Douglas, Lincoln repeatedly warned that Illinois itself might be turned into a slave state, with all the attendant evils, regardless of what her people wanted. The Constitution, as interpreted by the Supreme Court, was not the final authority, for there was a "higher law," the sensibilities of modern man, which ought to govern. "A house divided against itself cannot stand," proclaimed Lincoln at the start of his contest with Douglas for the Senate in 1858. "I believe this government cannot endure, permanently half slave and half free." Either the opponents of slavery would put it on the course to extinction, "or its advocates will push it forward, till it shall become alike lawful in *all* the States, old as well as new—North as well as South."

The Republican party emerged in 1856 as a coalition of disparate elements—mostly one-time Whigs, or Know-Nothings, with a large leaven of Yankee ex-Democrats from the northern part of the state who finally found a party consonant with their modern values. Also among the ex-Democrats in the new coalition were the more modern Germans, especially freethinkers and Protestants. The abolitionists in Illinois—that is, those who demanded the immediate, unconditional, uncompensated emancipation of all slaves—largely stood aloof from the new party, whose principles were simply not radical enough. This nonparticipation by abolitionists saved the Republicans much embarrassment as they repeatedly denied they would interfere with slavery in the South or with white supremacy in Illinois.

Propelled by the moralistic pietists in their ranks, the Republicans in 1856 crusaded enthusiastically against what they perceived as the demonic Slave Power. Methodist, Congregational, and Presbyterian pulpits rang with calls for Christian men to do their duty on election day. The Catholic Germans, denouncing the Republicans as "Temperance men, abolitionists, haters of foreigners, sacrilegious despoilers of churches, Catholic-killers," voted straight Democratic. In central Illinois Know-Nothings and ex-Whigs split three ways—most became Republicans, others tried to keep the American party alive, and the rest split their tickets between Fillmore (the American party candidate) for president and Republicans for state offices. Southern Illinois became solidly Democratic. Thus the Republicans lost the electoral vote of Illinois in 1856 but captured the governor's mansion, to remain there continuously for thirty-six years.

By 1858 the Republicans had a narrow majority in Illinois, thanks to continued immigration and the conversion of hesitant ex-Whigs. Because of the apportionment of the legislature, the margin was not enough to elect Lincoln to the Senate. Yet it was commonly acknowledged that in 1860 nothing could prevent a clear Republican sweep.

Despite the heated emotions, there was little violence. Douglas lost his temper in a letter to a Chicago newspaper in 1857, when he protested that Illinois might "be Yankeefied or Abolitionized, by freedom shrieking parsons and Abolition school teachers . . . those canting, shaffling demagogues who disgrace the pulpit and the schoolroom." Down in the southern third of the state, Republican partisans were but a tiny minority and few dared speak out. A delegation of masked riders threatened to lynch one man in Johnson County because he was outspoken for the Union cause, opposed slavery, favored prohibition, and had voted for Lincoln. He was saved when the mob discovered he was a fellow Mason; to the intense discomfort of his enemies he soon emerged as Lincoln's appointee as collector of income and liquor taxes. Elsewhere in Illinois some newcomers were torn by psychological crosspressures. A German immigrant in Joliet became involved in politics in the summer of 1860 when a friend asked him

Twenty times a day . . . was I for freedom or was I for slavery—and said I couldn't contradict that all men was born free and equal. He said the Democratic party was all for slavery, and that no one but Irish and Catholics belonged to it, and Douglas was a Catholic, and it was they that made the bad times and money scarce. He told me that every intelligent Dutchman belonged to the Republican party—for Abe Lincoln would make good times, money plenty, and the States all free.

So he joined the famed campaign group, the Wide-Awakes. He soon regretted it. "I lost more than ninety dollars for drinks and coal oil [for torches] . . . besides neglecting the business of my little store." After the election three of his debtors went broke because of falling corn prices, and he lost money on below-par banknotes. "If I had paid no attention to their blowing about freedom and slavery and freesoil, and minded my own business," he concluded, "I would be as much as $250 better off."

The Little Giant of American politics, Chicago's Stephen Douglas, had the courage of his convictions in speaking for traditionalist values against the Republicans. Hooted by his townspeople, denounced by Protestant ministers, and attacked by proslavery Democratic leaders in Washington, he rallied his forces, rebuilt his party, and won the Democratic nomination for president. Even more, he articulated a constitutional basis for the political principles of traditionalism: popular democracy. For Douglas, slavery was not the issue. He cared not whether it was voted up or down in the territories, so long as there was a free election. "Let the people speak!" He protested the homogenizing drive of both modernizers and the slave power. His vision was a nation of tolerance and diversity: a pluralism held together by white supremacy and the right of the people in their local communities to live as they chose, no matter how modern or traditional a lifestyle that might be. To him Yankee reformism—a melange of abolitionism, prohibitionism, nativism, and an intolerant sense of moral superiority—was a perversion of democracy to the extent that it forcibly tried to remold the perfectly good lives of traditional folk. The Catholics, who were the reformees in Illinois, cheered his vision. As for Dred Scott, Douglas dismissed it as a red herring. He explained in his debate with Lincoln at Freeport that slavery could never exist where the local population refused to protect it through police power and slave patrols. There was a deeper law more powerful than the Constitution, the Congress, and the courts: the support of the people at the grass roots, which determined the fate of any institution.

The third position, proslavery, was weak in Illinois.[1] As articulated by slave state spokesmen in Washington, it was posited on the primacy of property rights, specifically slave property. The Union was seen as a confederation of states, which retained basic rights, notably the right to establish slavery as a permanent institution. Other states, the Congress, the Supreme Court were constitutionally bound to honor those rights. If the North refused, it had broken the compact, and the slave states had the right to declare the Constitution a failure and secede to go their own way. In Dred Scott, the Supreme Court affirmed the proslavery argument on property rights, and the Buchanan administration went along willingly. The next affirmation of slave state rights would be expansion—not to inhospitable Kansas, perhaps; more likely to Cuba. Douglas's position was unacceptable because it exalted democracy above the right of the South to its way of life. The Republican position was unspeakable. In the 1860 election, Vice-President John Breckenridge carried the proslavery banner of the anti-Douglas southern Democrats. He carried most of the slave states but made no effort to win support in the North. In Illinois, Breckenridge won a few votes away from Douglas in Egypt, but not enough to affect the election. In Illinois, and in the nation as a whole, Lincoln would have carried the electoral college even if all his opponents had formed a coalition against him. They did not because they had as little in common with each other as they did with Lincoln. The decision of every northern state to give Lincoln its electoral vote proved to the South that the compact of Union was de-

1. The Episcopalian newspaper in Chicago printed a letter from a visitor to Virginia in 1859 who confidently reported that "nine-tenths of the slaves in the Old Dominion are infinitely happier and subjected to fewer privations than their free brethren in the North." As for slave auctions, the slaves "from their love of change and desire to travel, look forward with pleasure to being sold going South." Most Episcopalians opposed Lincoln.

stroyed. South Carolina promptly led the exodus to independence.

The fourth position, nationalism, reflected the practical businessman's nonmoralistic approach to modernity. Tennessee Senator John Bell made it his sole issue in 1860 as the presidential candidate of the ad hoc Constitutional Union party. Many ex-Whigs, particularly in the South and in southern Illinois, recalled nostalgically the leadership of Clay and Webster, whose timely compromises had staved off crises before. More practically, merchants, financiers, commercial farmers, planters, and railroad men feared the secession of the South would fragment the national market, disrupt trade channels, and ruin banks and other holders of southern state bonds, thus damaging economic growth. Since the Bell movement never got organized in the North, its Illinois admirers had to choose the lesser of two evils, Lincoln or Douglas.

At another level of consciousness, affection for the ideal of nationalism represented a modernizing stage wherein men had transcended localistic particularism. It was this latter sense of national identity that was challenged by the firing on Fort Sumter in April 1861. Illinois reacted in an outburst of patriotic fervor—the insult to the flag must be avenged! Douglas, who late in the presidential campaign began speaking more of nationalism than democracy, appealed to his followers to uphold the government. "This rebellion is a prodigious crime," he told the state legislature, "and the shortest way to peace is the most unanimous and stupendous preparation for war." His untimely death early in the war soon left more pacifistic, less nationalistic Democrats in control of their party.

Throughout northern and central Illinois, community leaders came together, without regard to party, to direct the aroused nationalism of the people into recruitment of troops, supplies, and money for war. Since the regular army was distrusted, and the militia system had long before disintegrated, soldiers were enlisted on a voluntary basis into state regiments. The governor gave out commissions for raising regiments to local political leaders, who used their network of connections to good advantage. Though an avid Republican, the governor at first gave commissions equally to Democrats, to acknowledge and confirm their patriotism. The companies and regiments elected officers on the basis of popularity and politics, rather than military skill. As a result the raw new army had to learn about soldiering the hard way.

Recruiting was easy in 1861—the glamour of being a soldier was irresistible to active young men; also, there was little fighting to do. The troops drilled endlessly, guarded bridges, occupied key points like Cairo at the junction of the Ohio and Mississippi rivers, and talked of a short, glorious war. In the spring of 1862 the fighting began in earnest, casualties mounted, and the war in the East became a series of disasters. Morale flagged, and the switch to three-year enlistments discouraged volunteering. Resentment rose further when the draft became law in 1862. Its purpose was to coerce men into enlisting, since only a few hundred Illinois draftees actually were forced into the army. Counties offered bounties—up to a year's wages—to meet their quotas, and Republicans redoubled their recruiting efforts. By late 1862, however, the growing Democratic opposition to the war effort made recruiting difficult, even dangerous. A couple of Illinois regiments were on the verge of mutiny; desertions ran in the thousands. The heavy demands for manpower late in the war might have led to open revolt had it not been for the large-scale enlistment of freed slaves into the Union army. Illinois sent a majority of its youth from eighteen to thirty-five to war—a quarter of a million in all. Casualties were relatively light—one man in twenty-five died in battle or from wounds. More dangerous was disease, which killed twice as many. Illinois troops suffered greatly from malaria, diarrhea, typhoid, dysentery; even measles became a feared killer under wartime conditions.

Despite the heavy drain in manpower, the homefront in Illinois and throughout the North expanded agricultural production to meet the demands of the army. Extra effort by farm wives, overage men, and underage youth, coupled with postponement of new improvements and routine maintenance around the farm made the greater output possible. Soaring food prices made it profitable. Money from crops and enlistment bounties funded the purchase of new laborsaving machinery, especially harvesting equipment. The continued rapid expansion of the state's rail network permitted more animals and crops to reach market faster and far more cheaply than ever before.

Manpower and food were the main contributions Illinois made. Its factories were too few and rudimentary to furnish cannons, rifles, or uniforms. Nor was the financial structure strong enough to absorb much of the heavy Federal debt. The people were able to volunteer their prayers and energies, however. Women took over farm duties, sewed uniforms, and rolled bandages. A few became nurses travelling with the army in the field; a somewhat larger number entertained the soldiers at brothels near Cairo, Springfield, and Chicago camps. More proper girls encouraged their beaux to enlist, or knitted socks for anonymous heroes on the battlefront. They might slip friendly messages into their offerings:

> My dear boy, I have knit those socks expressly for *you*. . . . I am nineteen years old, of medium height, of slight build, with blue eyes, fair complexion, light hair, and a good deal of it. . . . P.S. If the recipient of these socks has a wife, will he please exchange socks with some poor fellow not so fortunate.

In Egypt, sympathies with the South ran strong. If nearby Kentucky or Missouri had seceded, an effort to break away southern Illinois might have occurred. As it was, ugly talk about destroying bridges or raising brigades for the Confederacy was rampant. The outstanding leader in the region, Democrat John Logan, wavered, then finally announced for the Union cause and used his immense influence to recruit troops. State and Federal officials suppressed dissent by arresting Confederate sympathizers, closing hostile newspapers, and stationing troops prominently at key locations. Vigilante bands hunted down suspicious characters and deserters, driving dissent underground. In retaliation, guerrilla bands terrorized Unionists and discouraged enlistments. Bushwhackers, horsethieves, and desperadoes from Missouri threatened the river communities. As far north as Coles and Edgar counties bands of insurgents roamed, and in Charleston a full-scale riot against Federal troops occurred in 1864. Jonesboro, the center for marauders, was finally seized by Federal troops, who made mass arrests and by brute force guaranteed Egypt's loyalty to the Union.

War weariness emboldened the traditionalists to counterattack the alarming drift toward modernity. Taking control of a convention called to write a new state constitution in 1862, agrarian Democrats tried to destroy banks, stop railroad expansion, ban Negroes from entering Illinois, and gerrymander the legislature to prevent the growing northern regions from controlling the state. A fierce contest resulted in the narrow defeat of the proposed document. In the general election in 1862, however, the Democrats had better success, taking control of the state legislature.

The issue that most bitterly divided Illinois was the Emancipation Proclamation. Lincoln at first had tried to limit the war aims of the Union to nationalism, even at the cost of frustrating the more radical Republicans. His purpose was to keep the slaveowning border states from going over to the Confederacy. The proclamation freeing slaves behind Confederate lines was designed as a weapon of war, but it outraged Northern Democrats. The mass of Democrats would support a war only to restore "the Union as it was, the Constitution as it is, and the negroes where they are." By the fall of 1862 they were convinced that Lincoln had totally perverted these original aims. The suppression of civil liberties pointed to a military dictatorship. Rampant favoritism, profiteering, exhorbitant prices and blatant corruption on sales to the army disgusted even loyal Republicans. "The corruption and swindling in the army seems to be alarming," wrote one leading unionist. "Almost every Colonel who raised a regiment seems to have tried to make money by it." And, of course, with the war going badly the president received the blame. "How the butchers of antiquity sink into insignificance," thundered the Democratic paper in his hometown, "when their crimes are contrasted with those of Abraham Lincoln." Democracy, freedom of speech, honesty were all being destroyed, the Democrats felt. Worse, white supremacy was threatened. When the army began shipping trainloads of freed slaves from Cairo to points around the state, resentment reached fever pitch. Mass meetings denounced the abolitionists and warned that blacks would threaten free labor. "Do you that work in the shop, and you that strike the anvil wish the negro brought here to work beside you, to degrade labor and cheapen its pay?'' asked a Chicago orator. The upshot was the sweeping Democratic victory in 1862, and the threat that Lincoln would not be re-elected in 1864.

Republicans were in a quandary. Despite intensive support for emancipation by the modernizing pietistic churches, especially the Methodists, many Union men were frightened by the prospect of an Africanization of Illinois if hundreds of thousands of freed slaves would start coming from nearby Missouri and Kentucky. Radical Republicans likewise were disheartened with Lincoln's slowness and military reverses; they began plotting how to dump him from the 1864 ticket. Victory at Vicksburg and Gettysburg in 1863 raised Republican morale. Lincoln moved to shore up his position in his party by heavy use of patronage. By 1864 the Republicans were counterattacking vigorously. They defended emancipation by showing that black troops were fighting effectively—thus saving many white lives. Republican orators claimed that the freed slaves would not necessarily flock North. If the South were reconstructed to become attractive to blacks, they would ''skedaddle back to the sunny clime of Dixie'' and leave Illinois lily-white. Accusing the Democrats of harboring traitors, even of being secretly controlled by Confederate agents, the Republicans struck back hard. They pinned the epithet ''Copperhead'' indiscriminately on their political foes. Most important was the army itself. The soldiers overcame their racial bias when they saw how vital black troops were to their own survival and success. Writing home or visiting on furloughs, the soldiers condemned slackers and demanded wholehearted civilian support. Whatever their original politics, the vast majority of Illinois soldiers became staunch Republicans and ardent champions of the administration's policies. After the triumphant success of Lincoln and the Republican state tickets in 1864, it was inevitable that the total abolition of slavery would become a war aim, made permanent by the Thirteenth Amendment.

For four years Illinois men had shot, bayonetted, and blasted fellow Americans in the name of God and country. Strong, decisive action, no matter how brutal, illegal, or corrupt was easily justified; with the coming of peace it was hard to change abruptly. Politicians continued to call their opponents traitors or tyrants, and meant it. "Men cannot go through a prolonged emotional crisis and not pay the price," reflected Danville Congressman Joe Cannon, "It makes people hysterical." The bitter memories festered for decades. Old friends, alienated in the war, turned to insults, boycotts, false lawsuits, muttered threats. In Egypt the Republicanized veterans tried to ruin the stay-at-home Copperheads. Violent feuds erupted; in Williamson County alone three dozen men died in politically motivated assassinations between 1861 and 1874.

The parties were in disarray, groping for new leaders and new issues. Veterans established a powerful network of Grand Army of the Republic posts in towns across the state, and maneuvered to replace old guard Republicans with ribboned heroes. "One hundred soldiers of the late war have more influence politically, in any community, than two hundred citizens who never robbed henroosts or masticated Hard-Tack in range of Rebel guns," sputtered a frustrated Democrat. When Ulysses Grant of Galena became president the veterans took over hundreds of lucrative patronage jobs, and with them, control of the GOP. The new leaders had few compunctions about exploiting their power to recompense themselves for battlefield sacrifices. Later, the GAR would demand and get generous pensions for every survivor of the Union army. The original leaders of the Republican party were shocked by the widespread corruption, and by the blind party loyalty demanded by the new regime. The glorious crusade for freedom, the Lincolnian ideals that had nursed the movement in its heady days, had given way to waving the bloody shirt and crass opportunism. In 1872 the old guard launched its last crusade, this time against Grant and his cronies. They were crushed at the polls.

The Democratic party nearly disintegrated after the war. Tarred with the "Copperhead" stigma, the old leaders retired; young talent was slow to emerge and avoided state politics in favor of either private law practice or national politics. The Democrats had a powerful appeal to traditionalists in white supremacy and hostility to banks, railroads, commodity speculation, and monopoly. Without a new Douglas to orchestrate their plans, they threw their votes to any independent ticket that had even a remote chance of loosening the Republican loyalties of the majority. They even nominated prominent ex-Republicans who had been forced out of the GOP by the Grant coterie. Not until the 1890s, with Altgeld and Bryan, would Democrats find leaders to articulate the fear of being made obsolete by the onrush of economic modernization.

The moral decay that followed the war upset moralists across the state. The prostitutes, gamblers, and swindlers who had served the army camps adapted quickly to civilian life. Chicago counted two thousand "lewd women"; Cairo recorded a murder a week; and Springfield was overrun by "bullies, strumpets, vagrants and sneak thieves." Crime, including the white-collar variety, overwhelmed inefficient prosecutors and untrained police forces. "Defalcations, embezzlements, frauds, murders, swindles, violence, riots and thefts are and have been the order of the day," lamented the *Chicago Tribune* in 1875. Nor were rural areas immune. In White County between 1874 and 1882, one-eighth of the males eighteen to forty-five were committed to the county jail in Carmi. Half were convicted of larceny, burglary, forgery, or other crimes against property; a fifth were jailed for assault or murder; a fourth for concealed weapons, disturbing the peace, malicious mischief and the like; 7 percent were committed for rape, adultery, and bastardy. Deeper into Egypt the record was even more brutal. The fastest-growing item in the state budget was for building and maintaining penitentiaries and reform schools.

The Protestant churches, voicing alarm, renewed their efforts to combat drunkenness, family breakup, and sexual irregularity. To estimate the effectiveness of their efforts is problematical. In the early 1880s a survey of convicts at the state prison in Joliet showed 37 percent had been reared in a Protestant church (though only 17 percent were currently affiliated), and 33 percent had been brought up as Catholics, with the remainder innocent of Sunday school experience. However, two-thirds were orphans, of whom half had lost their fathers before age eighteen. The disruptions of war upon family life would exact their tolls for decades to come.

With the success of the antislavery crusade, the pietistic churches were left without a civic cause. Ministers thundered against desecration of Sunday by sports and amusements and condemned plays, dances, and card games as sinful as well. Noting the upsurge in drunkenness and the proliferation of saloons, they crusaded for prohibition. The formation of the Women's Christian Temperance Union in 1874 gave impetus to the movement. Success at the local level always seemed to distintegrate in the face of the unquenchable demands of German and Irish. Led by Evanston's Frances Willard, the WCTU turned to multiple reforms—including woman suffrage, rescue of prostitutes, censorship of pornography, and temperance education in the schools. Their efforts had considerable impact among the more modern youth in the state, but met indifference or hostility from the traditionalist Catholics and German Lutherans. Compulsory school instruction on the hazards of liquor and tobacco antagonized many parents; in Douglas County, the schoolboys "do not believe much of it." When temperance reformers won support from local Republican leaders, it was a signal for the Germans to start voting for Democrats. Consequently, victory-oriented Republican politicians managed to head off statewide prohibition no matter how unhappy this made the frustrated reformers.

The Civil War decisively shifted America, no less Illinois, toward faster modernization. The destruction of slavery spelled the defeat of forces in the South and in Illinois that most strenuously resisted the universalistic commitment to the equality of all men. To be sure, blacks were still not treated as equals, but the national commitment through constitutional amendments had been made. Further, the need to neutralize the white supremacy appeal of the Democrats led the Republicans to public avowal of equal civil rights for the blacks. For the next century the more modern middle classes, through their churches and politics especially, were nominally committed to civil rights and felt guilty when the reality did not match the ideal. Some of that guilt was overcome by the rationalization that blacks, by remaining very traditional, had not earned those rights.

A more general result of Union victory—Lincoln's special contribution—was renewed faith in America's mission to modernize the world. As the most advanced, most modern, most democratic nation, America had the duty to serve as a model for everyone else to follow. Lincoln had warned that disunion would "practically put an end to free government on earth." The failure of that model, mankind's best hope for a nation "conceived in liberty and dedicated to the proposition that all men are created equal" could never be tolerated. Victory had to be achieved without compromise. America had to dedicate its brains, muscle, money, iron, and blood to the proposition that "government of the people, by the people, for the people, shall not perish from the earth."

Lincoln's vision justified the horrors of civil warfare and lifted the horizon of the American people, eventually bringing them to the battlefields of Argonne, Okinawa, and Vietnam. The country would be ready for sacrifice, but remembering the terrible slaughter of the Civil War, insisted that the United States should always defeat its enemies by superior industrial might rather than by the death of American boys. This was the modern way of warfare, and it dictated strategy in all subsequent wars. Not until the frustrated aftermath of the failure of the American mission in Southeast Asia in the 1970s did people come to feel their society was so badly flawed that it was an unworthy model to impose upon the rest of mankind—that efforts to spread the gospel of modernization should be abandoned. But by then the entire core of modern values for which Illinois fought in the Civil War had come under question.

Politically, the Civil War made the modernizers dominant in Illinois by ensconcing the GOP in power almost continuously for seventy years. With its self-righteous appeal to morality, patriotism, and industrial growth, the Republican party secured the loyalties of pietistic (i.e., modernistic) church members, veterans, businessmen, and industrial workers. The Democrats' traditionalism held the loyalties of liturgical Catholics and Missouri Synod German Lutherans, antiwar elements, subsistence farmers, and unskilled farm and city laborers. Each coalition was strengthened by overlapping memberships. Thus most businessmen were pietistic in religion, and most Catholics were unskilled laborers. The liturgical or "high-church" viewpoint was that of most Roman Catholics and some Protestants who most prized orthodoxy and particularism. Central in their view was belief that the proper role of religion and the church was that of morality and orthodoxy, not social justice or secular politics. The pietistic or "low-church" type emphasized the ability of persons to have a direct, individual experience with Christ. Pietists were not so much concerned with rituals and creeds as they were with right moral action, including responsibility for reforming society. A sample of 11,600 voters in thirty-eight locations in six northern and central counties in 1877 shows how the overlapping memberships worked.

Three-fourths of the more modern pietists were Republicans, versus only a tenth of the heavily traditional liturgicals. Among pietists, the more middle class a person was, the more likely he was to vote Republican. Likewise for liturgicals. Thus modernity in religion added to modernity in occupation to produce very heavy Republican support. The pietistic businessmen were 80 percent Republican, and in a Methodist and Presbyterian town like Geneseo the rate soared to 95 percent. Conversely, traditionalism in religion added to lower-class occupational status to produce Democrats. A mere five percent of the unskilled liturgicals in the sample were Republicans. Men who were not churchgoers—about half the population—were Republicans or Democrats according to how modern their occupations were. The voting patterns made Republicans proud of their high status, as Democrats retorted defensively, "the men of the shops and of the farms, the laborers of the cities and the towns, in short, the workingmen, are the real owners of the country."

Rural Illinois communities had ceased to be isolated islands. The young men who marched away to fight in a dozen states returned with a more cosmopolitan understanding of the diversity and the potential of their country. War policy made in Washington, Springfield, or at army command posts affected every family and was closely followed through newspapers and the reports of travellers. Every man affiliated with a national party, listened to outside orators, was drilled both to vote the party ticket and to defend the party line. The offhand familiarity of the typical citizen with the niceties of tariff, monetary, or liquor policy amazed foreign visitors. The church members likewise belonged to cosmopolitan organizations. Theology and ritual were set by national assemblies; ministers were increasingly assigned from outside; missionary societies collected funds for faraway places. Even in daily life no one could mistake the changes. The age of

CHICAGO

A photographer's essay
by Donald Getsug

Photos in Sequence

Old and new buildings at Irving Park and Pine Grove.
Gold Coast residential buildings.
Resident of brownstone apartment near Old Town.
Advertising firm art director.
Inside Marshall Fields Department Store.
Police on the Gold Coast.
Doorman at apartment house on the Gold Coast.
Windows on the South Side.
Playing chess, Lake Shore Drive.
Picnickers, Lake Shore Drive.
Young people, Uptown.
Blues singer on Maxwell Street.
Suburban factory worker.
Pub near Lincoln Park.
Street scene at North Avenue and La Salle.

homespun was past, as families bought clothing, tools, machinery—even food—made in distant factories. Everyone realized that crop prices, railroad fares, the supply of mortgage money and credit, even farm wages, were determined not in the county seat but in national markets centered in New York or Chicago. The most unpleasant feature of farm life in the late nineteenth century was not cultural but geographic isolation. The roads were so bad that neighborly visiting had to be carefully planned and trips to the village limited to once or twice a week. Some women found an escape from loneliness in church meetings and Grange auxiliaries. They did not believe the myth of isolation producing insanity. Adolescents had the hardest time on the farm. "Nobody to see, nobody going by," observed a sociologist. "What is more natural than that the boys should get together in the barn, and while away the long winter evenings talking obscenity, telling filthy stories, recounting sex exploits, encouraging one another in vileness, perhaps indulging in unnatural practices."

The Civil War advanced the modernity of the Illinois economy. The small, wobbly state banks gave way to national banks, which provided the financial infrastructure necessary to negotiate complex commercial deals. The railroad system had proven its ability to ship huge quantities of food, equipment, and men at low cost. The state which measured only 111 miles of track in 1850 built 2,800 miles by 1860, 7,000 by 1875, and 10,000 by 1890. This increase in railroad mileage gave an enormous impetus to commercial grain and livestock farming, to coal mining (for fuel), car construction, hotels, and the wholesale trade.

During the war, young men from farms and villages learned to command military units in life-or-death situations and to coordinate the purchase and movement of supplies. After the war these skills were applied to business and farm management with striking results. In 1850 little manufacturing occurred in Illinois apart from numerous small gristmills. By 1870 rapid expansion was under way in a dozen industries, particularly those tied in with agriculture, such as meatpacking, flour milling, farm implements, and distilling. By 1890 Illinois had emerged as the third industrial state, with a quarter of the labor force engaged in manufacturing. Though most factories were still quite small, with only ten or twenty workers, attention focused on the giant meatpacking plants, steel mills, agricultural implement factories, and railroad car shops with hundreds, even thousands of employees. In 1900, seven of the country's twenty-two industrial plants employing more than 4,000 workers were in Chicago. Simultaneously construction, trade, finance, services, mining, and transportation grew in importance, absorbing nearly half of the labor force by 1890, leaving less than a third in agriculture.

Every city joined in the industrial boom. Peoria had distilleries, meatpacking and implement factories. Rockford specialized in furniture, machinery, and textiles; Joliet in steel; Moline in plows; Quincy in stoves; Elgin in watches; East Saint Louis in railroads, flour, meat, and chemicals. But the wonder city of the century soon came to dominate the state and the Midwest. "Big" was Chicago's watchword, noted the amazed architect Louis Sullivan.

> 'Biggest' was preferred, and the 'biggest in the world' was the braggart phrase on every tongue. Chicago had the biggest conflagration 'in the world.' It was the biggest grain and lumber market 'in the world.' It slaughtered more hogs than any city 'in the world.' It was the greatest railroad center, the greatest this, and the greatest that.

And, as well, had "the crudest, rawest, most savagely ambitious dreamers and would-be doers in the world." The Civil War takes much credit for Chicago's growth. The midwestern economy was modernizing rapidly, and Chicago's chief rivals, Saint Louis and Cincinnati, fell behind when their rural hinterlands were ravaged by war. Rich and poor, native and immigrant headed for Chicago to make money, to play out dreams. From 4,500 population in 1840, Chicago grew to 100,000 in 1860, 500,000 in 1880, 1,700,000 in 1900, and 2,200,000 in 1910—a growth rate so steep and so long sustained had never been seen in the world before. Of course, downstate grew too—from 1,600,000 in 1860 to 3,200,000 in 1910, largely because of the growth of towns and small cities.

Urbanization, industrialization, and modernization were not

the same phenomena in Illinois. The cities and towns established cultural, educational, and engineering centers to radiate modernity throughout the hinterland, but they also attracted vast numbers of European immigrants. Before the Civil War, an early sociologist noted, the average immigrant "was among the most enterprising, thrifty, alert, adventurous and courageous of the country from which he came. It required no small energy, prudence, forethought, and pain to come over." By the 1890s, the presumption was that immigrants were mostly very traditional: "it is now among the least thrifty and prosperous . . . that the emigration agent finds his best recruiting ground." More bluntly, reformers complained, "too frequently the immigrant is a European peasant whose horizon has been narrow, whose moral and religious training has been meager or false, and whose ideas of life are false."

Rhetoric like this underscored the uneasiness of the state's modernizers over the influx of hundreds of thousands of highly traditional peasants from Italy, Poland, Russia, Slovakia, Serbia, Greece, and other points in southern and Eastern Europe. The few modernizers in their midst often were revolutionary Socialists. Yet the unskilled labor of the immigrants was essential to the growth of the economy, as the meatpacking plants, steel mills, construction companies, and coal mine firms hired every able-bodied man who applied, whether he could speak English or not. Not until the 1920s, when the need for unskilled labor began to decline, were restrictions placed on the unlimited flow of immigrants into the United States.

The term "industry" conjures up visions of assembly lines, fast trains, and specialized services. But it also encompassed scientific, commercialized agriculture, and tradition-bound crafts. Modernity requires an eagerness for change, improvement, and efficiency. Illinois attracted and produced a growing middle class, whose members met the challenge, transforming the economy and the society while enriching themselves. The clash between modernizing impulses and traditionalistic resistance did not quickly or quietly disappear. Indeed, in the last quarter of the nineteenth century it appeared in new guises: the debate over compulsory schooling and the battle for control of working conditions waged between management and labor.

Education was a perennial source of tension between the modernizer, who thought it the perfect engine for the inculcation of his values, and the traditionalist, who, one educator complained, "got on right 'peartly' in his day with but a 'sprinkle' of 'them things' and his children can do the same." A bill to require all children from nine to fourteen to attend school three months a year died in 1874 when Democrats protested that it created "a new crime, to-wit: the crime of liberty in education." By the 1880s, rural children attended school only eighty-four days a year, and were mostly taught by untrained, inexperienced, teen-age girls. Only half the teachers had attended high school. "In too many cases," reported Iroquois County, "favoritism arising from social or religious affiliation, relationship, cheapness or mendacity . . . is a more potent factor in securing preferment as a teacher than worth." Although progressive communities prided themselves on the quality of graded and high schools, resistance was strong. "A school house is the worst possible investment this town can make," the *Monticello Bulletin* warned its readers in 1889. "Your children will not learn one iota more or faster. It will stop building, frighten away capital and keep the present taxpayers in the soup." Democrats wanted to exclude all "flub-dubs and fribbles" and considered high schools to be "tax eating monopolies . . . quasi colleges where dead and foreign languages were taught, and children are turned out expensive blockheads." Catholics resented paying taxes for "godless" public schools, especially resenting the pietistic tone of the modern educators. They expanded their own parochial system to include half or more of the Catholic children, who would learn the traditional rituals and beliefs of the church at the same time they picked up modern skills and self-discipline. The parochial schools were based on parishes, which in turn were based on ethnicity. Thus neighboring Catholic Irish and German children would attend different schools, with the latter taught in German.

In Chicago the educators saw their greatest challenge as "training children from homes of poverty and ignorance, if not of vice, to be honest, industrious and intelligent, and to adapt aliens to become active citizens." Despite shop and cooking courses designed to appeal to working-class children, the middle-class teachers were too strict in discipline, too hostile to traditionalistic behavior to attract students. Most working-class youth preferred factory work, because "they ain't always pickin' on you because you don't know things in a factory." One thirteen-year-old boy summed up the problem articulately: "They hits ye if yer don't learn . . . if ye whisper . . . if ye have string in yer pocket . . . if ye don't stan' up in time . . . if yer late . . . if ye forget the page." Not until the schools became attractive, the teachers competent and tolerant, and the drive for success more widespread did the traditional children attend one extra day they were not forced to.

In 1889 a Republican legislature passed the Edwards law, making attendance compulsory to age twelve, requiring basic instruction to be in English, and authorizing truant officers. Catholics were outraged at this intrusion into their cultural affairs as were German Lutherans, who also operated parochial schools. The Democrats took up a highly successful crusade against the law, and against the new McKinley tariff. In 1892 Chicago labor spokesman John Peter Altgeld barnstormed the German communities, denouncing the Edwards law as an intolerable example of Republican paternalism, of a kind with prohibition and nativism. The Republican promise to amend the law was worthless, he charged, because, "The spirit which enacted the alien and sedition laws, the spirit which actuated the 'Knownothing' party, the spirit which is forever carping about the foreign-born citizen and trying to abridge his privileges, is too deeply seated in the party." [2] Other Germans warned, "We soon would have a prohibition law, besides the Edwards law, to enslave us. . . . This campaign is a matter of life and death." The German vote swung heavily to the Democrats, and they elected Altgeld as the first Democratic governor in forty years.

The clash of modern and traditional work habits led to a large number of strikes in the late nineteenth century. Most active were low-skilled immigrant laborers in quarries, coal mines, lumberyards, and railroad track work. They were unable to form stable unions because they could be easily replaced by

[2] Altgeld's position was devious; he had participated in writing the Edwards law. He also tried to obtain a seat in the United States Senate by bribery in 1891.

other workers. Nevertheless, they struck frequently to secure higher wages and shorter hours. The appeal of the eight-hour day, which led to large-scale but short strikes in 1886, was to spread the work around and lower unemployment. The owners and managers strenuously opposed labor unions that might infringe upon their managerial responsibilities and lead to feather-bedding, absenteeism, and loafing on the job. When the labor market was tight, the strikes for higher wages often succeeded. Sometimes, however, management simply hired new workers and continued to operate. In an era before seniority, pensions, or fringe benefits, the strikers had little to lose.

Strikes and unions were both rare among the more skilled factory workers. The intricacy of expensive machinery and the complexity of the production process made strong foremen necessary. Indeed, foremen often operated as subcontractors with full responsibility. Punctuality, careful working habits, and reliability—modern traits—characterized most factory workers. Day wages—the norm for unskilled laborers—were too demoralizing for skilled and semiskilled factory employees. Piecework rates, which rewarded a worker strictly in accord with individual productivity, were more modern and more efficient. The employees accepted the system as an effective route to property accumulation. They came to identify politically with management and the Republican party, for they could understand how their jobs depended on protective tariffs, a stable financial system, and continued economic modernization. In 1876, 80 percent of the factory workers in Moline were Republicans. In 1896, secret polls of 9,800 downstate factory workers showed that 82 percent preferred McKinley.

Labor unions did flourish among skilled artisans—carpenters, typographers, railroad engineers, and the like. The unions provided fringe benefits and, more importantly, kept wages high by restricting the number of men who were allowed to learn the craft. Work habits were regulated by the craft and by tradition, not by overbearing foremen. Security was a major goal of the workers, and they were not threatened by technological innovation or other forms of modernization. Their unions formed alliances with the Democratic party. In 1896 the Democrats claimed that 90 percent of Chicago's union members preferred

Bryan. However, with fewer than 10 percent of the city's blue-collar work force enrolled in unions, they comprised a minor political factor until the New Deal.

The traditionalism of unskilled ethnic laborers, and their inability to form permanent unions or otherwise organize themselves frequently led to violent confrontations. The railroad strike of 1877, the Haymarket affair of 1886, the Pullman strike of 1894, and the coal strikes of 1894 and 1898 produced numerous deaths and injuries. When emotions flared high, destitution threatened, restraints were few, and the opportunities arose for settling personal grudges or expressing ethnic antagonisms, threats quickly turned to beatings, arson, looting, or shooting. Violence shocked the modernizers. They reorganized the National Guard after the 1877 riots, called for the execution of anarchists found guilty of inciting the violence at Haymarket, and supported the use of federal troops to reopen the railroads during the Pullman strike.

Governor Altgeld emerged as the hero of the traditionalists in the labor unrest of the 1890s. He pardoned the surviving Haymarket anarchists in 1893 with a stinging blast at the twisted sense of justice shown by the courts. He broke with President Cleveland and the small middle-class element in the Democratic party in 1894, denouncing the infringement of states' rights by the federal government in the Pullman strike. He then joined the free silver movement, and with William Jennings Bryan, crusaded in 1896 against the banks, railroads, insurance companies, industrialists, and federal courts. With Bryan running for president and Altgeld a candidate for re-election as governor, the traditionalists presented a formidable ticket that year. The country was in the fourth year of a severe depression—unemployment was very high in the cities and farm prices were severely depressed. The crusaders identified the cause of the hard times with the selfish greed of the modernizers, and promised a cleansing of the temple, a return to a simpler, more just, safer economy. "When I preach to the common people deliverance from the money changer," Bryan told a Chicago audience, "I preach to the businessman deliverance from the tyranny of the bank. . . . The big criminals should wear striped clothes as well as the little criminals." The intensive proselytizing shook old loyalties. One Springfield Democrat exclaimed that scores of Republicans "have come forward like sinners in a religious revival and joined us with public denunciations of their old party affiliations."

The modernizers counterattacked furiously. Free silver was immoral, they warned the thrifty folk, because it would produce runaway inflation that would deplete savings accounts and insurance policies. Bryan's program would quickly bankrupt the railroads, do nothing to restore factory employment, and raise prices faster than wages. To top it off, Bryan and Altgeld were wild men in league with anarchists, and allegedly stood opposed to every modern value cherished by the middle classes. In a positive vein, the Republicans argued that a sound financial system, based on the gold standard, coupled with a high protective tariff to screen out foreign imports and encourage the building or reopening of American factories, was the only way to achieve recovery. William McKinley made a special appeal to traditionalist German voters, promising a benevolent pluralism and no more pietistic crusades against their beer gardens, parochial schools and other cultural institutions. Indeed, Bryan appeared as the fiery crusader, just like those prohibitionists and nativists who for so long had bothered the Germans.

The 1896 election was the most intense political contest in Illinois or American history. Nearly everyone voted, and the results were decisive. McKinley ran up massive majorities among the more modern ethnic and occupational groups in Illinois. He carried 65 percent of the Yankees, 70 percent of the British, 80 percent of the Dutch, and 75 percent of the Jews. The huge German vote in the state veered sharply toward the GOP. In German wards of Chicago where Altgeld won 62 percent of the vote in 1892, he and Bryan dropped to only 42 percent in 1896. Only the most traditional ethnic groups, Irish and Polish Catholics, voted heavily Democratic. "The Republican ranks consist practically entirely of rich monopolists, who are robbing the poor people," explained the *Dziennik Chicagoski,* the leading Polish newspaper in the state. "Shall we then, plain workingmen, entrust offices to them and in this manner help them to continue to oppress us? Go hand in hand with our old friends, the Democrats; that is our only salvation."

Downstate the results were mixed. McKinley carried the towns and cities, and a majority of the commercial farmers. But some tenants and the marginal farmers swung toward the Democrats. The net result was a solid Republican majority, soon made permanent by the return of prosperity just as McKinley had promised. Not for thirty-six years would any Democrat win a majority of the state's vote.

Bryan exhorted agrarian traditionalists, regardless of partisan, ethnic, religious, or cultural background, to join his crusade against modernity. Rural Illinois rejected his appeal in 1896, and the similar Populist call in 1892 and 1894, because corn belt farmers had achieved a high level of economic and cultural modernity, and were not disposed to go backward. To appreciate this development we must review the condition of agriculture in the northern two-thirds of the state (the corn belt), with special attention to the deceptively simple question of who became landowners.

Before the Civil War, prairie farming was equally land speculation, subsistence food growing, and commercial crop production. Before the settlers arrived, speculators had bought up most of the land from the federal government, the Illinois Central Railroad, the state, or other speculators. The slickest operators, working on borrowed money, accumulated thousands, even tens of thousands of acres for a few dollars an acre, intending to make a fortune when the surging westward movement of population drove up land values. Many fortunes were made—and some destroyed—in the process. Early arrivals with an eye to the main chance, but with little cash, set up claim clubs that coerced latecomers to pay off the extralegal "claims" before buying the land from the government. (The homestead law, it should be noted, came too late to affect Illinois.)

A settler who wanted to purchase a small eighty-acre prairie farm in 1850, would need to pay $1,500 for land, buildings, fences, livestock, seed, and implements. A transplanted New Englander or a German immigrant might have the cash from selling out back home. Bank loans or mortgages were hard to find, but speculators and railroads were willing to sell on five-year contracts. A man with only a few hundred dollars could rent land, using his capital for livestock and implements. Those

without money would have to start as hired laborers at $10 or
$20 a month plus room and board; a fourth of Illinois farmers,
chiefly young men, were laborers in 1860.

The 36 million acres of land in Illinois were enough for a
quarter of a million farms. The westward tide filled them rapidly: one-fourth by 1850, half by 1860, nearly all by 1875. The
rapid growth of the state's railroad network, and the steady fall
in freight rates, opened a national market for Illinois foodstuffs.
In 1870, three-fourths of the farms were within five miles of a
railroad, and only 5 percent were more than ten miles distant.
The result was a dramatic upsurge in land values, from $8 an
acre in 1850, to $20 in 1860, $30 in 1870, $54 in 1900, and
$108 in 1910. The equalitarian society of pioneer days could not
survive in the new market-oriented economy. In 1850, as we
have seen in the last chapter, very few farmers were worth more
than $2,500, and the disparity in living standards between the
richest and poorest thirds was not great. Already by 1870 the
change was dramatic. Thirty percent of the farmers were landless and held less than $300 in personal property, while the
richest third had a minimum of $3,000 in real estate, plus more
than $1,000 worth of equipment, furniture, and savings. "We
dislike to see so many good people leaving [Piatt] County for
Iowa," editorialized the *Mansfield Express* in 1896, "but the
land is so valuable here and rents high that men of moderate
means cannot afford to live."

Prosperous landowners and more ambitious tenants rapidly
modernized their operations during and after the Civil War. High
prices meant good profits for the man who produced for the
market. The traditional system of concentrating first on food for
the family, then selling any surplus, gave way to commercial
agriculture. The modernizers bought newer, improved implements, fenced their land with barbed wire, installed tile to drain
the wet lands, replaced slow oxen with more efficient horses,
enlarged their herds of cattle and hogs, sought improved animal
breeds and seed, and switched from wheat (which was easy to
grow) to the more lucrative combination of corn, hogs, and
cattle. They let none of their land lay idle, and hired young men
to handle the extra chores. They formed Granges to exchange
ideas and competed at county fairs to see whose innovations

were the best. The wealthiest owners sent their sons and daughters to high school and even college, and prepared for the day when they could retire in comfort on lucrative rents.

Illinois farmers were strongly opposed to breaking up their holdings. Only one child would inherit the farm, but he or she would have to pay the other children a fair price for their shares. Average farm size stabilized at 120 to 130 acres—the optimum size for the technology of the day. The landless children, after a spell working as hired hands or teachers, would either have to find another farm or move to an urban job. A detailed study of Iowa youth gives us some insight on what became of Illinois youth in the same circumstances about the turn of the century. Sons of farm owners stayed on the land 73 percent of the time— with 35 percent becoming owners and 35 percent renters (many of these eventually became owners). The rest found urban white-collar (14 percent) or craftsman (8 percent) jobs; very few became farm laborers (3 percent) or urban laborers (6 percent). The sons of renters were less successful. Only 18 percent became farm owners, 39 percent renters, and 6 percent farm laborers. A larger fraction, 37 percent, found urban jobs, either white-collar (15 percent), craftsman (12 percent), or unskilled labor (6 percent). With Chicago and Saint Louis more accessible, it seems likely that a somewhat higher proportion of Illinois than Iowa youth went to the big city. Other studies of corn belt farm owners in the early twentieth century show that two-thirds worked their way up the farm "ladder"—as hired hands or tenant farmers before becoming owners at age twenty-nine to thirty-six. Half of this group obtained their land through inheritance, marriage, or arrangement with relatives. The other third of the owners never were hired hands or tenants. At age twenty-six or so they inherited the family farm.

The implication of these studies is clearly that mobility in rural Illinois was becoming frozen by the 1890s: few men would own land unless they inherited wealth or married the daughter of a landowner. Bryan's prescription for rural relief therefore was irrelevant. He focused on inflating crop prices. Since this would quickly raise the cost of a farm, it would be of little help to the tenant farmer saving to buy land. Traditionalist land owners, especially in the southeastern part of the state, who still empha-

sized subsistence agriculture and had little use for modern techniques, saw they would benefit from a rise in land values, and
in the export price of their wheat; they voted for Bryan. The
modern farmer, however, had no intention of selling his land,
and would not benefit directly from farm inflation. His profit
came from food sales to the city; he listened to Republican
warnings that Bryan's free silver panacea would bankrupt the
railroads and impoverish the urban market. Modernized farmers
had no use for Bryan and voted heavily Republican.

The Republican triumph in 1896 sealed the victory of the
modernizers in Illinois politics. Henceforth there would be no
serious debate on the desirability of a fully modernized economy. Only a small minority of Socialists would continue to call
in question the desirability of a capitalistic society oriented toward maximum use of natural and human resources for rapid
growth. True, concerned citizens in the early twentieth century
debated whether bankers, railroad magnates, and industrialists
exercised too much power over small businessmen, or ignored
the health and safety of their employees and customers. These
issues were raised in order to improve the overall level of economic modernity in Illinois, not to reverse its progress.

4

Prosperity in Farm, Town, and City: 1900–1930

$\mathcal{A}$FTER 1896 prosperity returned to America, and Illinois farms, mines, mills, shops, stores, and offices enjoyed the rewards of economic modernization as never before. The steady growth in American urban population and wealth produced a heavy demand for Illinois beef, pork, milk, horses, and oats. Farmers continued to mechanize and enlarge their operations to meet the new opportunity for rapid profits. An acre of corn, which had produced a tiny profit of 83 cents in the late 1890s, yielded an average of $8 profit by the eve of the First World War. Land prices rose accordingly. The average farm, which had been worth $6,100 in 1890, was valued at $7,600 in 1900 and an amazing $15,500 in 1910, about $100,000 in 1978 dollars.

The farmers' new wealth spilled over into the towns and cities of downstate Illinois. Small towns grew by providing transportation, merchandise, finance, education, and personal services to agriculture. Small cities enlarged their factories, deepened their coal mines, upgraded their railroad shops, and raised wages all around. Merchants beamed at the long rows of Model Ts lined up on Main Street on Saturday night; ministers heard the tinkle of prosperity the next morning.

Chicago's mighty boom—continuous since the 1840s, with but a pause during the depressed 1890s—spiralled upward until

1929. To the million inhabitants in 1890 another 600,000 were added by 1900, another 500,000 by 1910, and yet another 1,200,000 by 1930, when the total finally levelled off at 3,400,000. Just behind Berlin and ahead of Paris, Chicago was the fourth city in size in the world, and second in wealth only to New York. The manufacturing and transportation base of the city's economy continued to flourish. Chicago's banking, commerce, and services (like law, medicine, education, entertainment) dominated the entire Midwest, leaving Saint Louis and Detroit far behind. Only the "Big Apple"—New York itself— could be a fit comparison for grandeur, wealth, and power. Despite the heavy influx of unskilled immigrants, the city's occupational force was steadily upgraded. White-collar jobs grew much faster than blue-collar ones; after 1920 the numbers of unskilled laborers and servants shrank drastically. Chicago's escalating land values typified the optimism of the one city that saw all the wildest dreams of her founders fully realized.

The twentieth century brought an end to the physical isolation of rural Illinois, opening the villages and farms of the state to ever-more-rapid cultural and economic modernization. In the late nineteenth century, travel for more than a few miles was extremely difficult. Horse-drawn wagons and buggies, churning through deep mud in spring, choking dust in summer, and snow drifts or deep frozen ruts in the winter, seldom could travel more than six miles an hour. Given the need to feed and rest the animals, the result was that a round trip of twenty miles or more required an overnight stay. A visit with friends or kinfolk was an all-day or even weekend affair requiring advance planning. Country students had to find room and board in town if they wanted to attend high school. Trips to the city were rare events. True, a fine railroad network honeycombed the state, but passenger service was expensive and the problem of making connections, sitting through layovers, and renting livery at the destination drastically limited the amount of casual travel possible by rail. Rural Illinoisans simply stayed home, save for weekly ventures to little villages for supplies.

Two technological innovations broke down the isolation. The first was the electric interurban railroad, which flourished between 1900 and 1925. It provided fast, inexpensive travel between towns, opening up vast hinterlands around Chicago and Saint Louis. By 1925, however, the interurbans lost out to the automobile and the scheduled passenger bus. Today only the South Shore commuter line, linking Chicago with Gary and South Bend, survives of this once-proud system.

The automobile first appeared as a rich man's toy. As late as 1909, the newspaper in a small town south of Rockford reported with amazement, "The automobile traffic through Oregon Sunday was tremendous, something like over a hundred machines passing through the streets on that day." Seven years later a traffic survey counted 1,065 automobiles coming through the town in one day, together with 82 motorcycles, 24 trucks, 37 horse-drawn wagons, 177 carriages, and 4 men on saddle horses. The automobile, thanks to Henry Ford's Model T, was now cheaper to operate than a horse, and far faster, safer, and more convenient, and less polluting.

The automobile created a demand for good roads. After 1913, when the state government began sharing the expense of building roads, highway construction became the major activity of state and county government. Paved roads lifted Illinois out of the mud. Farmers could truck their crops and animals more cheaply to market, so they willingly paid the higher taxes. Motor trucks soon took over much of the freight business from the railroads. By 1927, 90 percent of the downstate families owned an automobile. Short, casual visits replaced the all-day affair. Farmers and villagers discovered how easy it was now to dash off to town for a movie or for shopping. Intercity high school football and basketball contests became major social events for the community, while the students themselves created new uses for the privacy afforded by the auto. Villages lost much of their economic function. Small- and medium-sized cities with their superior shopping facilities crowded out the old general store. Rural workers discovered they could commute to jobs in a wide radius, making the young folk even less willing to plan on a life in agriculture.

Rural isolationism crumbled further with the rapid expansion of telephone service to outlying areas and the girding of the state by electric power utilities. By 1927, half the downstate housewives had a telephone, and two-thirds had electricity. Indoor plumbing and new appliances—better stoves, refrigerators, sewing machines, irons, washing machines, vacuum cleaners— made for easier and more efficient housework, and removed the need for domestic servants. Farmers owned more and better equipment, which enabled them to produce more at the same time they were cutting down on hours of labor. The abundant new leisure that resulted led to more relaxation, more community activities, and more schooling for the children. The circulation of national magazines soared, while newspapers waxed fatter with more features, more advertising, more local news, and less dull political reporting. Best of all, the people spent their leisure in relaxed, quiet evenings enjoyed in larger, better-furnished, warmer homes.

The transportation revolution took a different form in Chicago. In 1890 the city's million inhabitants travelled chiefly on foot—not difficult, since a majority lived within three miles of State and Madison. Only the homeowning, outlying middle classes spent their money on the horse-drawn street cars. Few but the very rich owned a horse and carriage. By 1920, the city had tripled in size. The inner ring, already overcrowded in 1890, grew not at all. The new dwellings were four, five, even ten miles from the Loop. Although factory workers and unskilled laborers still walked to work, the rapidly growing middle classes depended on public transportation, especially the rapid transit ("el") system that made it feasible to buy or rent in a pleasant neighborhood while working downtown. By the late 1920s the more affluent middle classes had established themselves in suburban Cook County. They owned automobiles for pleasure and shopping but usually commuted to work by rail. Not until after the Second World War would the ownership of cars by Chicago's working classes permit the diffusion of factories and large stores into the suburbs.

Prosperity and sustained economic growth attracted millions of people to Illinois, creating a diversity of lifestyles and cultural values that could scarcely be matched anywhere in the world. Class and ethnicity, viewed along the spectrum from more traditional to more modern, increasingly stratified the population into distinct, hostile groups.

The lower class, composed of criminal elements and the very

poor who experienced frequent family disruptions and economic hardships, grew rapidly. As outlaws, horse thieves, and pillagers were driven from the rural areas, an urban underworld swelled in size. Red light districts flourished in every city, reaching world-famous proportions in Chicago's near south side. Rows of cheap saloons, day labor hiring halls, flophouses, brothels, pawnshops, and gambling joints lined the fast-expanding slum districts. The poorest of the poor, including drifters from all across America, immigrants from Italy and Southern Europe, and blacks escaping peonage in Dixie, crowded into dank, stinking tenements. Employment was haphazard—hard, unskilled day labor for men, servant or laundry jobs for women. Wages were miserably low. Malnutrition was normal; tuberculosis threatened everyone; child mortality was frightful. Hygiene was ignored by both the superstitious, fatalistic folk and the corrupt municipal officials. Welfare and relief came not from the government but from luckier relatives, an overburdened voluntary charity program instituted by the upper classes, and, most often, from neighborhood politicians and saloonkeepers who traded bushels of coal and free lunches for the votes that spelled political power in the city.

The poor trapped in the slums were not criminals, yet their children quickly learned what sort of man flashed a diamond ring, what sort of woman sported fancy gowns and feathery bonnets. Boys who stole fruit and coal because their families were hungry and cold gravitated to gangs for companionship and illicit excitement. The more stable gangs, patronized by astute politicians, set up clubhouses and athletic clubs, became somewhat respectable, and often emerged as political forces. So long as industry craved unskilled labor, and tens of thousands of peasant immigrants flocked to the metropolis to pick gold from the streets, the lower class grew in size. The immigrants from Southern and Eastern Europe were mostly men, who intended either to send for their wives later or else return to the native village rich, with perhaps $500 in cash. Meanwhile they crowded into boardinghouses or lodged with workers' families. Despite low wages they saved up to half their incomes, wealth that brought respectability for some, dangerous entertainment in the red light district for others. The outbreak of European war in

1914 ended the mass influx of peasants, enabling those trapped in America to take advantage of high wartime wages and to adjust to the city. Prosperity and experience helped the poor rise to stable working-class status, while the criminals discovered that Prohibition had created a new, incredibly profitable industry that rewarded men of force and ruthlessness.

Above the lower-class slumdwellers were the more stable blue-collar working classes. Low-skilled and unskilled factory, construction, railroad, and sanitation workers with relatively steady jobs formed the bulk of the working class. They were immigrants, or the sons and daughters of traditional peasants, from Germany, Poland, Bohemia, Slovakia, Ireland, Lithuania, the Ukraine, and a dozen European lands. After a decade or more in the United States they had developed stable family lives, based on male supremacy, strong kinship ties, and devout religious practice. The more successful men, semiskilled and skilled factory workers, craftsmen, police, and firemen, had perhaps accumulated some savings, or even purchased a bungalow. They aspired not so much to middle-class status for themselves or their children as to security in an era of fluctuating unemployment and unreliable banks. Over the course of a lifetime of effort, perhaps a fourth of the workers would rise to a more secure, higher status white-collar job, such as storekeeper, foreman, or self-employed artisan. Another tenth might become skilled craftsmen. The vast majority would depend all their lives on manual labor and the uncertainties of the industrial business cycle. Save for the depression years of 1893 to 1896, wages were high, and rising relative to the cost of living. The material aspirations of the workers could be achieved by years of hard work, careful budgeting, and the luck to avoid a disabling accident or long illness. Old age was feared less because of the threats of senility or ill health, than of financial insecurity and dependence.

Above all, the working class sought to avoid the degradation of pauperism and crime. Even though their youth might belong to gangs, and the unmarried men might frequent brothels, bookmakers, and boxing matches, and all men socialized in saloons, the working classes were more often the victims than the perpetrators of burglaries, robberies, and muggings. Politically, the working classes were closely allied with the machines, either Democrat or Republican depending on the city, the neighborhood, and the particular ethnic group involved. Labor unions became a permanent factor in working-class life only in the late 1930s. Before then, unions had sporadic strength, sometimes waxing strong (coal miners, teamsters, printers, garment workers), then collapsing. Only the construction craftsmen, the elite of the working classes, were able to sustain strong unions continuously. The factory workers, at the other extreme, were usually nonunion.

Culturally the working classes participated in church rituals. The women were especially devout Catholics. If religion were a nominal affair back in the old country, good only for christenings, weddings, and burials, in America it was an anchor for a person's identity—ethnic awareness and social life both emerged from the church and synagogue. Other Old World cultural traditions gradually disappeared in America. The young people spoke English and could hardly sing the old songs or understand the folktales grandfather wanted to tell. Folk costumes were a huge embarrassment, except on certain festival days when it was all right to dress funny. Ethnic organizations like the Czech Sokols, German Turnverein, or the Slovenic National Benefit Society were chiefly middle class in leadership, with a modest working-class following. The chief fellowship most men knew was a circle of friends at the corner saloon, or relatives gathered for family celebrations.

The increasing modernity and complexity of the economy caused the ranks of the middle class to expand even more rapidly than the working class. The wholesale and retail trades hired thousands of young men and women as clerks, bookkeepers, and salespersons. Banks, insurance companies, railroads, and schools needed well-educated, reliable accountants, tellers, teachers, typists, and junior executives. Employers demanded modern skills for these white-collar jobs. Quickness at reading, writing, and arithmetic, together with alertness at handling abstractions and poise in dealing with customers or co-workers and above all, reliability, were the requisites that reserved white-collar positions for men and women who had internalized modern, middle-class norms. Few immigrants, and no more than one in three children of blue-collar families, qualified for white-collar jobs and entry into the middle class.

White-collar employment carried far more prestige and benefits than blue-collar jobs. Although the starting pay was about the same, the young man with a white collar had distinct advantages. Office work was cleaner, easier, and more pleasant than manual labor. More important, there was far more job security and chance for advancement to high-paying managerial posts. Furthermore, the skills developed in the white-collar work could easily be transferred to private life. The middle classes dominated the leadership and active membership of almost all clubs, societies, churches, and community groups. In turn, they supported the expansion of the public school system, especially the high schools, to inculcate modern values and thus further to swell the ranks of the middle class. Women found teaching and office work far more enjoyable and prestigious than blue-collar factory or servant jobs. While few middle-class women expected lifetime careers, their jobs gave them the chance to meet up-and-coming young men, get married, and move to comfortable semisuburban homes.

Comfort was the great discovery of the middle classes. Good nutrition, hygiene, warm homes, clean water, sewers, and access to modern medicine made the middle-class family healthy and vigorous. Servants were cheap and easily available before the First World War, providing free time for the employer and training in needed skills for the servants. Expensive new household appliances and conveniences made cooking and cleaning much easier for the middle-class housewife than for the poorer working-class wife, who still had to scrub clothes, lug water, and tend to more numerous, more sickly children. With her leisure, the middle-class woman could read, sew, and pour her energies into church activities and woman's clubs. Middle-class men likewise had far more leisure and security than blue-collar counterparts. Better housing, better clothing, better medical care, better transportation, safer neighborhoods, occasional vacations, and greater involvement in voluntary societies were the rewards of middle-class occupations.

Thanks to the evangelical fervor of their churches—

Methodist, Presbyterian, and Congregationalist, especially—the middle classes felt a sense of duty to uplift those less fortunate than themselves, those more traditionalistic in lifestyle. They subsidized foreign and home missions, organized youth groups, supported civic beautification, public health, and the public schools. Poverty—save for the old and sick—was caused by the lack of modern values, they believed. Abolish the saloon, the brothel, the gambling hall, require compulsory schooling, end child labor, destroy the corrupt political machine, and all would be right with society, they believed. The social settlement, like Hull House, manifested these values perfectly. The Roman Catholic Church, with its mysterious rituals, shadowy priests, and "un-American" parochial schools, seemed more a threat than an acceptable denomination to many middle-class Protestants. The more cosmopolitan, however, understood that the Catholic community itself contained a growing middle class, committed to modern values, sexual purity, and uplift of its own sort for the immigrants. After 1916, George Mundelein, the Catholic archbishop of Chicago, worked to modernize his elaborate network of schools, hospitals, and charities. Efficiency, centralization, and resistance to ethnic particularism made him an outstanding modernizer. The growth of benevolent societies like the Polish National Alliance or Unione Siciliana testified to the rise of a middle class in the ethnic communities of the state.

Astride the highest reaches of society and economy in Illinois was the upper class—a powerful cluster of wealthy real estate magnates, lawyers, physicians, bankers, merchants, professors, and corporate executives. They took pride in owning Chicago and in controlling everything of importance except city hall and the Catholic church. Downstate also had its dominant clans— the Deere-Butterworth and Hauberg-Denkmann families in the Quad Cities, for example, or the Funk-Stubblefield family in McLean County, the Stevensons in Bloomington, and the Bradleys in Peoria. They were enlisted in every civic enterprise, sat on the boards of banks and industries, and built museums, hospitals, and schools.

Nowhere in the Midwest did the upper class shine as brightly as Chicago. Fabulous fortunes in manufacturing, transportation, retailing, banking, and—above all—real estate, gave the city a hundred millionaires by 1900. It was an era when a million dollars implied a great mansion on Prairie Avenue, the Gold Coast, or Lake Forest, complete with carriages, artwork, and a host of servants. The Armours, Fields, McCormicks, Palmers, Pullmans, Rosenwalds, and Ryersons entertained lavishly, mesmerizing the readers of the society pages with their latest comings and goings. The nice thing about Chicago was that unlike the East, a famous family name was not a requisite for entry into high society. Only money and vigor.

Much more important than fancy dress balls or ornate Parisian gowns were the civic, cultural, and political activities of the very rich. By the time of the 1871 fire, if not earlier, the upper class had decided to make Chicago the cultural capital of America, perhaps the world. The effort nearly succeeded. Two decades after the fire, raw, burgeoning Chicago staged a world's fair that left the world agog with its stunning display of sophisticated architecture and learning. Overnight the city built the greatest university in the United States, and libraries, an art institute, a symphony orchestra, and a natural history museum that surpassed anything outside New York, with the gap closing rapidly between the two cities. To complement the institutional monuments, Chicago acquired a galaxy of outstanding novelists, critics, poets—and even a few painters and sculptors. The metropolis became a cultural center that could never be ignored by the most snobbish easterners.

The dazzle of Chicago's high culture came from its daring, even audacious appropriation of European achievements. Like the Japanese industrialists in the 1960s or the Arab oil sheiks in the 1970s, Chicago's rich had the cash to buy the best there was. The Art Institute assembled French masterpieces, the Newberry Library hunted out the rarest and oldest books, the orchestra performed the finest German music, and the opera brought in outstanding Italian singers. The very buildings which housed the great art and learning were copied from old European originals. Chicago now possessed splendid showcases for the opulence of her captains of finance.

Truly creative vigor in art could not be bought. It had to emerge from the genius of the people. The upper class did make gestures in this direction. Yet the orchestra found no Anton

Dvořák in the city. Efforts to encourage handicrafts and folk art among the working classes foundered; only the well-to-do found satisfaction in stone-carving, furniture design, and the fine binding of books. The outstanding art in Illinois took the form of social criticism—ranging from heavy-handed exposés of the squalor in packingtown (*The Jungle* of Upton Sinclair) to delicate character studies of the decay of moral values (Theodore Dreiser's *Sister Carrie*). Apart from a few upper-class poets, the best writing was a product of close observation of life in the streets and the slums of the working classes. Journalists, steeped in the argot of sports, politics, crime, and scandal led the way. Carl Sandburg, James T. Farrell (*Studs Lonigan*), Peter Finley Dunne (*Mr. Dooley*), and later Richard Wright (*Black Boy*), Nelson Algren, and Studs Terkel excoriated the rich and celebrated the poor, the ethnics, the workers.

The final irony of the failure of upper-class culture to take root in the city could be seen in music. The opera, fantastically expensive bauble of the very rich, went bankrupt with the onset of depression. Chicago's world-famous music came not from the imposing concert halls in the Loop, but from the bordellos and speakeasies of the black South Side. There the blues and jazz of New Orleans and Memphis reached perfection in the inspired and improvised sounds of bandleader King Oliver, pianist Earl Hines, and trumpet virtuoso Louis Armstrong. Benny Goodman abandoned his musicology studies at Hull House to play in dance halls, picking up the black rhythms and arrangements that made him the "King of Swing" to white audiences everywhere.

In one arena the high culture did triumph: architecture. Chicago dazzled the world with its ingeniously planned world's fair in 1893, and sustained its leadership with great skyscrapers that caught the beauty of steel, glass, and concrete. These structures housed the business offices that powered the Midwest. (Curiously, the city's great libraries, churches, museums and universities were modelled after European architectural monuments, and thus contributed little to Chicago's leadership in the field until the 1950s.) By forming discreet alliances with the politicians, the civic leaders among the elite secured wide-range city planning that built up the lakefront parks, the boulevards, and the forest preserves. The crash in 1929 put a stop to grand construction for a quarter-century, when new money restored Chicago's leadership in the world of architecture.

As the middle class lost interest in partisan politics, the upper and lower classes moved to fill the vacuum, particularly in Chicago. The elite was overwhelmingly Republican, save for a handful of Catholic Democrats. The McCormick family provided leadership in the pages of the *Chicago Tribune,* and in the person of Senator Medill McCormick. Frank Lowden, wartime governor and presidential aspirant in 1920, was Pullman's son-in-law. In tune with the civic reformism popular among the elite, McCormick, Lowden, and the *Tribune* led the progressive wing of the GOP. They were opposed by traditional ethnic politicians operating full-scale machines in different parts of the city.

Upper-class efforts to modernize the culture and lifestyle of the working classes went beyond art. Nowhere in the country did modernizing schemes proliferate as fast as in Chicago. Compulsory education, settlement houses, voluntary charities, YMCAs, even philanthropic housing complexes were the chosen instruments. The elite created civic reform groups, vice and crime commissions, and manual training institutes; they also fostered high schools and Americanization classes. When these failed to transform the working classes they subsidized sociological research at the University of Chicago to analyze the causes of deviance, poverty, disorder, and corruption. To no avail. The ethnics and working classes rallied to William H. ("Big Bill") Thompson, who systematically insulted the elite; he even formed an alliance with Al Capone's criminals. In desperation the elite and the middle-class reformers threw their support to Anton Cermak, leader of the wets and the new ethnics. Cermak finally destroyed Thompson and helped suppress organized crime while building a new Democratic political machine that was anathema to reformers for decades to come.

Downstate Illinois was suspicious of the paternalism and reformism of the Chicago elite, preferring instead practical, lower-middle-class art, useful colleges, nostalgic memorials, and Republican machines. Uncle Joe Cannon, congressman from Danville for a half-century and powerful Speaker of the

House, was their type of leader. Downstate built up the University of Illinois as a middle-class counterweight to the elite University of Chicago, and Urbana wisely confined its creative genius to engineering, agriculture, home economics, and library science. Save for the medical school, all the state institutions of higher education were kept out of the Chicago area, to forestall elite control. Springfield developed a Lincoln legend to guide downstate back to a rustic heritage of the sort Carl Sandburg celebrated so well. Chicago, where power was divided between the upper and lower classes, thus became increasingly alienated from middle-class downstate, a tension that kept the city from full self-government, which in turn saved it from the sort of extravagance that bankrupted Detroit in the 1930s and New York in the 1970s.

The Main Street vision of the Good Society in Illinois concerned itself with modest, utilitarian enterprises. The prosperous lawyers, physicians, ministers, bankers, landowners, and merchants who controlled local government could easily envision the advantages of a new post office, park, old people's home, water purification plant, or high school in the daily life of their community. Their own families would use them first. The local leaders first computed the impact on their tax bills; they were not extravagant. Not threatened by an inundation of uncontrollable, dangerous foreign peasants, they created neither monuments to their own wealth nor instruments for transforming the working classes. The schools and churches they built were for the benefit of their own children. They were open, too, for those ambitious offspring of the working class who overcame the peer group pressure to renounce "sissy" schoolwork. The middle classes knew their children would drift to the cities. Before they left, they would internalize the values of Sunday school, Christian Endeavor, the Boy Scouts, and Central High School. With a high school diploma, perhaps even the experience of a spell at Knox or MacMurray or the state university, they would move easily into the well-paid managerial and professional ranks in Chicago, Peoria, Rockford, or Saint Louis. The sinful lures of the saloon and brothel would not divert their children from the comfortable family life and rewarding careers that were possible in Illinois.

After the dizzy series of upheavals and tumultuous political excitement in the 1890s, the people of Illinois began to shed their intense partisanship. Eventually the result was widespread apathy. In the first two decades of the century, however, the total fervor that once roused men to party devotion continued to blaze among the more modern voters but became channelled into progressive reform. Each party and politician espoused "progressivism" on at least a few issues, though no one battled consistently for every progressive measure that came along. Three styles of progressive reform emerged: crusades against corruption; crusades for social welfare; and systematic drives for efficiency and the modernization of government. Crusaders against corruption were middle-class farmers and townspeople who feared that illegitimate power blocs (bosses, parties, giant corporations, labor unions, unresponsive judges) were becoming dangerous threats to the emergence of the good society in America generally, and Illinois especially. The "malefactors of great wealth," as President Theodore Roosevelt called them, together with corrupt politicians, had to be destroyed by an aroused, outraged citizenry before it was too late.

The crusaders for social welfare included social workers, ministers, philanthropists, labor leaders, and some of the more modern ethnic politicians who sought to use the state's legal power to ameliorate the harsh conditions in slums, factories, and shops which might prevent the lower classes from enjoying a minimum standard of living and eventually shedding their traditional habits and folkways. The third group of efficiency-oriented progressives were experts—physicians, educators, engineers, architects, lawyers, and managers—who saw the time had arrived to jettison old-fashioned practices and modernize institutions, especially government, in accord with the scientific principles of the new age. The three groups were often in agreement on the goals they sought for Illinois, though the persistence of traditional party organizations in the state legislature and in city halls as often as not frustrated their specific projects.

The crusaders identified traditional party organizations, buttressed by partisan loyalty, patronage, and the very complexity of the ballot, as the first obstacle to the permanent triumph of the reform ethos. They responded with direct election of senators and direct primaries, designed to circumvent boss control; and with registration laws to prevent fraud and inhibit ignorant voters. Woman suffrage became law in Illinois in 1913, not so much as an acknowledgment of female equality in the political sphere as a weapon to enlarge the ranks of the moralistic voters. Since middle-class women turned out at the polls in far greater numbers than more traditionalistic ethnic women, the cause of crusading reform was well served.

Reform never admitted the possibility that politicians could compete to provide good government. Municipal government, reformers felt, had to be depoliticized to be efficient, so they advocated city manager and commission forms. These were adopted successfully in homogeneous modern towns and suburbs. In larger cities these reforms became battlegrounds between the civic-minded, cosmopolitan middle classes who held there could be only one best way to do things, and localistic, ethnic, and union-oriented workers who felt their particularistic needs would be overlooked. In Rock Island it literally took a gun battle before the reformers drove out the old regime. In Peoria the middle classes lacked unified leadership and structural reform failed. In Chicago the politicians and ethnics were too well organized for the reformers. In Rockford, Yankee, Scandinavian, and German reformers overthrew both major parties and governed the city with an economy-and-efficiency oriented Socialist party for thirty-six years.

Civil service was the ultimate weapon to destroy the old politics. Modern criteria of tested merit, certified experience and formal credentials replaced the traditional methods of personal influence, family connection, or partisan reward as the routes to government appointments and promotions. Chicago, in an early burst of progressive reform, adopted a civil service law in 1895, and was followed by Evanston, Springfield, Waukegan, and other cities. The machine found enough loopholes—like "temporary" appointments outside the merit system—to be able to tolerate the law. In 1905 the state government switched from spoils to civil service; governors soon discovered they had little patronage to distribute. Since the federal government already had abandoned the patronage system, the parties lost their best lure for avid workers. Only county government continued to use political influence as the basis for jobs, contracts, and favors. Such traditionalist devices helped maintain courthouse cliques, especially in rural Illinois, and kept the state legislature in the hands of professional politicians long after the parties lost their central role in government.

As early as the 1920s, the bureaucracy had taken control of routine government in Illinois. Filling out forms properly, going through channels, and standing in line replaced a word with the precinct captain as the way to get a building permit or a license plate or a welfare check. Whether the frustrations and aggravations occasioned by the bureaucracy outweighed its superior efficiency and honesty was never questioned by the middle class. The bureaucracy, as the creature of the cost-conscious middle class, did not reach out to the poor who especially needed help. In Chicago, the political machine retrained its precinct workers as ombudsmen who advised the bewildered on exactly how to deal with the government. Middle-class groups, such as veterans' and farmers' organizations, worked energetically to guarantee that all members received all the government benefits to which they were entitled. Only in the 1960s, as part of the nationwide war on poverty, were the poor canvassed in order to learn who was eligible for welfare benefits.

Social welfare progressivism fared poorly in Illinois. Humanitarians and labor leaders constantly called for laws to enhance worker safety, protect women workers, abolish child labor, enact public health measures, and eliminate slums. The less controversial proposals, chiefly public health programs (vaccinations, hospitals, pure water) were enacted easily. Child labor was abolished early, in part because labor unions did not want the competition. Nevertheless, when newspapers pointed to the "business skills" their boy carriers learned, and farmers extolled the healthfulness of outdoor labor, those occupations became exempt from the most restrictive child labor laws. Labor legislation was successful chiefly when it appealed to the ethic of efficiency. Thus miner and factory safety laws were passed and enforced. The number and severity of accidents suffered by railroad employees dropped 90 percent between 1914 and 1934, while the rate of accidents in coal mining fell by half. Railroads and some corporations set up pensions to rid themselves, in a humane way, of supposedly decrepit old men. Industrialists vigorously opposed most of the legislation proposed by labor unions, fearing that their management responsibilities would be undercut, and that featherbedding would inevitably result. Not until the New Deal and the enactment of federal legislation would minimum wage and maximum hours come to Illinois, or labor unions win the guarantee of collective bargaining, or the old, blind, poor and unemployed receive halfway decent benefits.

The issue of worker benefits touched directly on conflicting modern versus traditional perspectives on wealth. The traditionalist view, held strongly by many workers and by labor unions, conceived of a fixed economic pie that should be divided equitably, with workers deserving more in the form of wages than employers allowed. The moderns emphasized the importance of economic growth—making the pie larger—and stressed the need to channel wealth through the hands of expert bankers, entrepreneurs, and investors, lest the economy stagnate. In times of depression, when the promise of economic growth soured, the traditionalist view gained strength, and proposals to tax the rich and redistribute wealth won adherents. In times of prosperity and rapid growth, far fewer people were willing to risk upsetting the system. Local government, state as well as county, committed until the 1970s to raising revenue from relatively regressive property, sales, tobacco, and liquor taxes, was never in a position to significantly redistribute wealth within the state. That was mainly a federal matter, and thus entered state politics only indirectly.

The most bitter crusades waged by the progressives impinged directly on the ethno-cultural forces in Illinois. Prohibition, pitting the moralistic, middle-class pietists against the traditionalistic working-class liturgicals, was fiercely contested. The WCTU, headquartered in Evanston, lost its role as the spearhead of the dry forces around 1900, when the Anti-Saloon League took charge. The league mobilized the major Protestant churches, especially the powerful Methodists, Disciples of Christ, Presbyterians, Baptists, and Congregationalists. A vote for or against candidates blessed or damned by the league became a test of Christian citizenship for a million voters. The wets counterorganized in Chicago and Peoria, led by the liquor interests and a coalition of ethnic groups formed by Chicago's mayor-to-be, Anton Cermak. The wets may have outnumbered the drys in Illinois, but many were immigrants unable to vote. With the convergence of wartime anti-German antagonism and the final push by the drys, Illinois ratified the Eighteenth Amendment and passed its own state-enforced prohibition statutes in 1919, thereby officially closing 7,000 saloons in Chicago, 300 in Peoria, and 220 in Springfield.

The ideals of science, expertise, professionalism, and a disgust with fraud, waste, and old-fashioned inefficiency motivated reformers to define new powers for the major professions in society. The physicians, acting through medical societies and state licensing laws, upgraded medical education, controlled the availability of powerful drugs, and drove quacks underground. Educators used certification, county teacher institutes, and normal schools (which eventually became state universities at DeKalb, Carbondale, Bloomington, Charleston, and Macomb) to improve dramatically the qualifications of schoolteachers. Dentists, lawyers, veterinarians, pharmacists, and college professors raised the prestige of their professions by formal licensing laws, improved professional schools, and cohesive guilds whose regular conventions mixed sociability with an exposure to new ideas and the latest techniques. The model was infectious: barbers set up "colleges," secured state licensing, and dreamed of middle-class status for tonsorial professors.

Outstanding success rewarded the efforts of physicians, public health officials, and sanitary experts to improve the health of Illinois. One baby in four born in the 1880s died within a few weeks of birth, chiefly from intestinal disorder or pneumonia. By the 1920s, the proportion was down to 7 percent—much higher in slum areas—and today it is barely 1 percent. Pure milk in urban areas was the major factor. Reformers forced through laws requiring inspection of dairies, pasteurization, and destruction of diseased cattle, despite much grumbling. Malaria faded away as an endemic disease in the late nineteenth century as swampy lands were drained for crops. Crowded slum conditions in the late nineteenth and early twentieth centuries made tuberculosis the leading cause of death in the state. Badly pol-

luted drinking water supplies, lack of garbage pickup, and absence of sewer systems made typhoid fever and diphtheria major
scourges in the late nineteenth century. Chicago took the lead in
combatting these contagious diseases by installing adequate sew-
age and water systems, setting up laboratories for diagnosis,
requiring cases to be reported to the board of health, and employing nurses to instruct immigrants in the vital need for cleanliness. By 1930, these tactics had proven successful and the
death rate from infectious disease plunged to minimal levels.
Only poliomyelitis proved resistant to the combination of public
health measures, improved sanitation, and scientific diagnosis.
After the Second World War, the appearance of penicillin and
other antibiotics finally wiped out tuberculosis and reduced the
danger of pneumonia. New vaccines in the 1950s eliminated
poliomyelitis, and infectious disease no longer posed a major
public health problem—except, that is, for venereal disease,
which increased steadily toward epidemic proportions despite
the availability of antibiotics and systematic public health measures, such as free clinics and widespread testing.

The overlap of concern for social welfare and business efficiency found expression in the personnel policies of large Illinois corporations in the first thirty years of the century. Previously, most employers followed the traditional practice of
letting foremen have complete control over hiring, firing, wage
rates, and work speed. George Pullman tried a new tactic in the
1880s, building a model community for his workers, but other
businessmen were dubious. "The fact is," concluded the president of the Chicago, Burlington and Quincy Railroad in 1886,
"the more you do for your men, outside of paying them good
wages and treating them with proper personal respect, the more
they want." After defeating a bitter strike in 1885, however, the
railroad began an accident-sickness insurance program to head
off further union threats. By the first years of the century most
railroads had adopted retirement pension plans, and the Illinois
Central was experimenting with an employee stockholding
scheme.

Inspired by the advice of Jane Addams and other social workers, International Harvester, Western Electric, U.S. Steel, and
the meat packers began large-scale efforts to improve working

conditions in their Chicago area plants. Safety devices, sanitary facilities, lunchrooms, emergency medical care, and better ventilation increased worker productivity. Morale was improved by setting up night school courses in shop skills, arithmetic, and English, and by sponsoring clubs and recreations. To cut down on wasteful turnover, savings banks, death benefits, pensions, and profit-sharing programs were begun. Smaller companies, like the *Chicago Daily News,* remained paternalistic, providing employees with a Christmas turkey or a gold watch on retirement. But large corporations, especially those with many clerks or skilled craftsmen, such as Sears, Roebuck, Commonwealth Edison, and downstate utilities went further and set up house magazines, ended seasonal layoffs, and subsidized purchase of company stock. By inculcating white-collar employees with a team spirit, industry developed a more loyal, more efficient, and more stable work force and headed off any chance of unionization.

Large employers of low-skilled labor modernized their labor relations by shifting hiring responsibility from the foremen to a personnel office, which after the First World War often used psychological tests and medical examinations to guarantee the fitness of new workers. Night school classes proved an effective technique for upgrading the labor force, or at least for introducing the men to modern industrial discipline. Those studying English at International Harvester learned to read: "I hear the whistle. I must hurry. I work until the whistle blows to quit. I leave my place nice and clean." In 1912 U.S. Steel began showing a movie about an ignorant, stupid Hungarian peasant who becomes a forward-looking, industrious workingman thanks to the company's safety and welfare program. The benevolence was not all charity. Employee welfare work, explained an International Harvester executive in 1909, would "so knit its vast organization together, would so stimulate initiative, would so strengthen and develop the *esprit de corps* of the organization, as to make it possible for the company to increase its business and its earnings."

The climax of progressivism was America's entry into the Great War (no one was so cynical as to call it the First World War at the time). Before 1917 Americans recoiled in horror at the incredible folly of European civilization draining its blood—at the rate of ten thousand lives every day—in a conflict that seemed so purposeless. Neutrality in thought and deed was the dominant mood. The close cultural ties between citizens of British and German descent and the mother countries produced noisy propaganda battles and quiet efforts to lend aid. German and Austrians in the Chicago area raised a million dollars for humanitarian aid to be distributed through the German Red Cross. Irish Catholics gave moral and financial support to the rebels in Dublin and fiercely denounced the British for their suppression of Irish freedom. British sympathizers, however, dominated the cultural, educational, and financial pinnacles in Illinois, and used their influence to sway elite public opinion toward the Allied cause. Samuel Insull, the utility magnate of Chicago, himself an immigrant from England, used his wealth, his corporate connections, and his boundless energy secretly to help Americans enlist in Allied armies, to manipulate press opinion, and to channel loans and gifts to the British. Less effectively, Socialists and humanitarians, especially Jane Addams, proclaiming peace as the highest goal, rallied their supporters to protest any American involvement.

Germany's deliberate violations of America's neutral rights on the high seas finally led to a declaration of war in April 1917. With cold fury, President Wilson proclaimed a crusade to make the world safe for democracy, to end the cruel, aristocratic militarism and imperialism that threatened to destroy liberty in the world. Quickly, opinion leaders in the state caught the theme. The leading Republican newspaper in Springfield, abandoning partisanship for a while, echoed Wilson:

> We will fight fair, we will honorably live up to all our agreements and we will kill and destroy as mercifully as possible. But the decision must be such that hereafter no nation will dare to resort to unrestricted slaughter upon the world's seas which the Creator gave to all men in common that they might rise above the beasts and become brothers.

The war became a crusade to modernize the world—to smash the reactionary threat and install the rule of law, the spirit of democracy, the love of liberty everywhere. Governor Frank Lowden, an articulate Republican with presidential ambitions, criss-crossed the state proclaiming that Germany was "the cruelest military autocracy the world has ever known," embodying "all that civilization thought it had conquered years ago." America fought the "holiest cause" ever, a re-enactment on a world scale of the Civil War against slavery. The contest pitted individual liberty, democracy, and righteousness against the suppression of human rights, against the "Anti-Christ." To mobilize the people to the cause scholars wrote learned studies of the rapacity of the Hun, storekeepers waved flags, thousands of patriots scouted out spies, saboteurs, and draft evaders. That everyone should understand the great crusades, Chicagoans devised the "Four Minute Men" movement early in the war. A thousand orators in the fraternal section, twelve hundred in the church section, and six dozen in the labor union section worked with twenty-eight hundred "regular spellbinders" to enumerate war aims, sell war bonds and stir up patriotism before every possible crowd, assembly, or gathering. The Illinois audiences numbered 800,000 a week and quickly the idea spread nationwide.

Lowden entrusted day-to-day supervision of the war effort to a new quasi-public body, the Illinois Council of Defense, headed by Insull. Outstanding industrialists, labor union officials, educators, and women's leaders made up the council, and volunteers from the Insull electrical empire efficiently organized operations. The council mobilized every resource in the state for total war. Public opinion was galvanized; industry, finance, and transportation were co-ordinated; coal prices were rolled back; fraternal orders, church groups, and charities were taught to co-operate. Schools were transformed into engines of war, with the universities training officers, the high schools drilling prospective draftees, and the grammar children distributing leaflets and learning how to economize at home.

Slowly America recruited an army for the final assault on Germany; more than a third of a million Illinois men, half draftees and half volunteers, prepared for battle. Mercifully, the Armistice came before too many had to die. America's greatest contribution to winning the war was neither weapons nor cannon fodder—which reached the battle fronts too late. Instead, money and food to sustain Britain, France, and Italy were the vital resources. Money proved easy to raise; food was the challenge, especially for the state which dominated the nation's breadbasket and distribution center. "The last battle between the forces of evil and the forces of righteousness," the governor waxed eloquent, "will be fought, not on the battlefronts of Europe, but in the wheat fields, the corn fields, in the gardens, and in the feed lots of Illinois." It proved difficult to expand farm production overnight, despite the soaring crop prices. The war cut down the supply of agricultural labor and agricultural implements despite favorable draft board rulings and the hectic mobilization of city youth for farm work. The solution was to economize on waste, to cut back on consumption. Hundreds of thousands of housewives took emergency lessons in food economy and learned to prepare menus without meat and wheat one day a week. Coupled with staggering increases in food prices, these measures released enough foodstuffs to meet the quotas and win the war.

Grumblings about wartime prices and shortages threatened civilian morale. One of Chicago's Czech newspapers complained:

> Of what use is it if we raise vegetables in our back yards to help agricultural production—of what use are all the appeals to the public to support our food administration, if the war profiteers, unconscionable speculators, and other parasites hoard food only to let it rot rather than lower prices?

To meet the criticism, the government increased its appeals for conservation, cracked down on speculators, raised corporate taxes to confiscatory levels, stepped up Americanization programs to modernize instantly the ethnic workers, and sent its investigators to learn whether saboteurs were spreading these ugly rumors. The federal government refused to impose rationing or price controls, for the voluntary food program was working as well as could reasonably be expected. The federal government did, however, nationalize railroads, coal mining, shipping, telephones, and telegraph communications for the duration of the war to guarantee that these vital services would operate without breakdown.

Labor posed a question mark early in the war. The unions harbored strong antiwar socialist elements, raising the possibility of sabotage. State and federal government responded by co-opting union leadership, and tolerating prowar socialists while systematically and ruthlessly suppressing the pacifist wing. Anti-war spokesmen were jailed, their newspapers shut down, their rallies broken up by police and National Guard troops. Only in Bloomington were antiwar sentiments expressed by union leaders. In return for their co-operation and for an informal ban on strikes, unions received gains they had long dreamed of: wages shot up faster than inflation, the eight-hour day was man-dated (despite the resulting loss of production), and employers in coal, steel, and meat were forced to accept unionization of their labor forces. Income taxes were raised, but with high enough exemptions that few blue-collar workers had to file a re-turn.

Industry's rapid conversion to the war effort, and the sudden end of European immigration, created a severe labor shortage, which further raised wages, but which also led to the importa-tion of large numbers of southern blacks into Chicago and East Saint Louis. With housing scarce and racial tensions high, vio-lence was inevitable. The worst outbreak came in July 1917, in East Saint Louis, where the reputation of blacks as strike-breakers and corrupt voters and the tense emotionalism pro-duced by the draft, rising food and fuel prices, and anti-German propaganda, overcame the feeble efforts of an utterly corrupt municipal administration to keep order. Whites attacked, stoned, shot, and murdered dozens of blacks, until National Guard troops arrived finally to restore quiet. With everyone afraid that the expanding black belt in Chicago would explode next, the legislature made it a criminal offense to incite race or religious prejudice. Chicago black leaders assured whites that they were desperately trying to avoid trouble: "We advise our people not to sit by whites in the [street] cars, to avoid white restaurants and theaters; not to intermarry or to live in white dis-tricts." Miraculously, Chicago remained calm until the war was over.

America mobilized psychologically by transforming a mili-tary conflict into a crusade for modernization and for American-ism, and, at last, into a race war. Not against the colored races, to be sure; against the Huns. Germany was vilified as the arch-foe of everything America stood for. It was an easy step—and psychologically an inevitable one—to identify an enemy at home as more insidious than the Boche hordes in the trenches. At first the enemies were spies, saboteurs, slackers, pacifists. Soon it became any institution, or even name, identified with Germany. French courses replaced German in the high schools. Sauerkraut easily became liberty cabbage; German shepherd dogs transformed themselves into Alsatians without barking back. Street names could be changed; Bach, Mozart, Beethoven, Wagner, and Brahms dropped from musical programs in favor of more suitable, if less talented, English and French composers. Frederick Stock, the brilliant conductor of the Chicago Symphony Orchestra—itself founded by a German—resigned his post until he could take out citizenship papers. But what was to be the fate of less prominent German-American citizens?

Illinois was the center of German settlement in America, with Chicago its cultural headquarters. Ten million Americans were one, two, or three generations removed from Germany—one million of them lived in Chicago, Peoria, Quincy, Belleville, and scores of towns, villages, and rural areas across the state. Declaration of war stunned these quiet people. There was no concerted action by the diverse community. Some became superpatriots, affirming their loyalty to America by taking the lead in destruction of everything Germanic in their culture. Others quietly voted for Socialist antiwar candidates or dared join in rallies broken up by the police. The vast majority kept a low profile. The federal government suppressed the Socialists, closed down ethnic newspapers that had questioned the wisdom of war, and closely censored the rest. All suspicious German Americans came under surveillance, and all German community leaders came under suspicion. There were in fact no spies or saboteurs, yet fears and accusations flourished wildly. State and federal officials monitored enlistments and bond subscriptions in German areas to detect slackers or the slightest hint of disloyalty. When bond sales lagged in the heavily German rural areas of western Cook and Du Page counties, the district attorney ordered Lutheran ministers to lecture their congregations on their duty to God and country.

Where suasion or threats failed, ruder tactics took over. In Carlinville, in the central coal fields, a German was arrested for spreading the canard that the Red Cross sold sweaters to dough-boys, and for suggesting that the German army might not have committed all the atrocities credited to it, indeed, that American soldiers under pressure might conceivably react cruelly, too. He was lucky. The next day a mob dragged his cellmate—a free-talking antiwar German Socialist—out of the jail and lynched him. National, even international attention focused on the in-cident, and the governor denounced the crime. No one was punished, but the government did step up its suppression of "enemy sympathizers" to forestall further mob violence.

With its antiwar spokesmen jailed, and the neutrals harassed, the proud German-American community in Illinois verged on disintegration. A measure of the intensity of hatred was the rapid ratification of Prohibition, on the new grounds that Ger-mans controlled the breweries and saloons, and their influence must be crushed. "It is a war of *destruction!* Annihilation is its aim!" protested the leading German publisher. "Under the plea that it is necessary to defeat the Kaiser," he explained, "the German language is to be tabooed, every man and woman of German stock and name is to be made a despised pariah, and left to the tender mercies of any bloodthirsty mob, or any scoun-drel, who uses the Stars and Stripes to hide behind." [1] When German voters reacted by voting Socialist, the *Chicago Tribune* darkly warned that such unpatriotic conduct "will be cherished against German Americans in all walks of life for many a day, and . . . is not going to be beneficial to German-Americans ei-ther in their business or their social relations."

The harassment Germans suffered did not compare with the relocation of West Coast Japanese in 1942, or the jailings of Confederate sympathizers in the Civil War. Almost immediately after the Armistice, the hysterical emotions unleashed by the na-tional crusade shifted abruptly away from Germans toward radi-cals and Bolsheviks, as though the wartime hatred against loyal

1. Paul F. Mueller to Sen. J. Hamilton Lewis, April 6, 1918, in Cole Notes, Illinois Historical Survey. This candid letter had to be private; publication would bring a five-year prison sentence. Quoted here with permission of Illinois Historical Survey, University of Illinois Library, Urbana.

citizens had never existed. The Germans forgot very slowly. Fearing the wrath of their neighbors might some day recur, they abandoned their distinctive foreign-language newspapers, poetry, and church sermons. Lutheran and Catholic parochial schools began to use English exclusively, with the children taught to think of themselves only as Americans. Confidence in government would not be restored for many years. Germans voted overwhelmingly against the Democrats in 1920 and for third-party candidate Robert LaFollette in 1924 (since he had opposed the war). When war with Germany again loomed in 1940, midwesterners of German descent cringed in dread of another ordeal and voted heavily for antiwar Republicans.

The German community in Illinois had always been inwardly directed, avoiding Yankee politics, Yankee churches, Yankee society. They created their own intellectual, religious, social, and artistic institutions, supported by the modest wealth of their hard-working, loyal people. The wartime hysteria destroyed a flourishing culture in Illinois, replacing it with the sullen fear and frustration of cynics. The war to modernize the world, to spread liberty and democracy, left the homefront strewn with invisible casualties, unseen wreckage, and lingering bitterness.

The world knows Chicago as the capital of crime and violence. Indeed, a thousand movies cannot be all wrong. In the 1920s, deliberate, calculated violence and syndicated crime raged unchecked in Chicago, in industrial suburbs like Cicero and Joliet, and in downstate cities, especially in East Saint Louis and in mining towns. The record is staggering. Even apart from weird episodes like the Leopold-Loeb "perfect murder," Illinois experienced violence that shocked modern men and women everywhere. Spectacular race riots, with whites savagely attacking and murdering blacks, exploded in Springfield in 1908, East Saint Louis in 1917, and Chicago in 1919. Scores of people were killed, hundreds injured, tens of thousands frightened and embittered for decades. Gang warfare killed scores of "little punks" and "big dealers," culminating in the Saint Valentine's Day Massacre of 1929. From 1926 to 1930, some two hundred men were slain in gang killings, with all the gory details lavishly reported by press and motion pictures. Only slightly less spectacular was labor violence. In the big cities, racketeers in trucking, dry cleaning, and entertainment shot up their competitors. The coal fields, always wide open and bloody, witnessed a cold-blooded massacre of two dozen strike-breakers at Herrin in 1922, and years of pitched warfare be-tween rival mine unions that even the National Guard was un-able to control. Nor was politics immune. While assassination never became a major threat to civil order, frequent threats, bombings, and an occasional murder frightened public men into a realization that violence was a central fact of life in Illinois.

The most striking characteristic of the violence of the 1920s was not its volume, but the failure of the government to combat it. The situation was very different from the 1970s, when an epi-demic of homicide, rape, aggravated assault, mugging, bur-glary, and armed robbery made hundreds of miles of city streets and many apartment buildings dangerous at night and unsafe by day. Random, personal crime of this type existed in the 1920s, but at rather lower levels of intensity, and there was no large class of drug users whose addiction absorbed hundreds of thou-sands of dollars every week. The cities of the 1920s, particu-larly Chicago and the coal towns, were rough places, scenes of frequent brawls, knifings, and robberies, especially in the flourishing red light districts. The average person, however, could easily avoid the dangerous areas if he or she wished. What the citizens could not avoid, particularly the newspaper-reading middle class, was a humiliating awareness that the gov-ernment co-operated with big-time hoodlums, while it enforced the law against juveniles, petty criminals, and careless au-tomobile drivers.

The corruption existed at the highest levels—the mayors of Chicago and East Saint Louis, the state's attorney office in large counties, even the governor's mansion were linked through payoffs and political alliances with bootleggers, labor racke-teers, gambling syndicates, brothels, and street gangs. The cor-rupt alliances involved both political parties; most surprisingly, the Republicans—the party of morality—were more deeply tainted than the Democrats. In Cook County and statewide, cor-rupt Republican machines had overpowered both the elite and the middle-class moralists by effective use of ethnic voting blocs, timely alliances with Democratic ward leaders, and unstinting use of patronage. Not until the late 1920s, when Big Bill Thompson's Republican machine was at last defeated in Chicago by a coalition of elites, reformers, and Democrats, did the middle-class moralistic Republicans regain control of their party. The cost, politically, was high, for by the mid-1930s the Democrats in Chicago had absorbed most of the Republican strength in black and working-class ethnic neighborhoods. The middle-class Republicans were never able to win in Chicago, and the city passed permanently into the hands of a newly built and virtually invincible Democratic machine.

Two of the most traditionalistic groups in Chicago, the Italians and the blacks, provided the basis for much (about half) of the large-scale syndicate crime in the 1920s and 1930s. Al Capone symbolized the era rather well. The Italians—together with Irish Catholics and Russian Jews—constituted the great majority of syndicate leaders, racketeers, bootleggers, kidnappers, extortionists, bodyguards, bondsmen, and small-time hoodlums. They made up less than a third of Chicago's population and accounted for only a small proportion of the "petty," unorganized felons sentenced to the state penitentiary. The city's large German, Slavic, Yankee, and Scandinavian populations were significantly underrepresented in the ranks of organized crime, according to careful secret studies undertaken in the late 1920s by sociologists. At the same time, the ranks of Chicago law enforcement—police captains, assistant state's attorneys, bailiffs, and judges—were dominated by Irish Catholics, with proportionate numbers of Yankees, Germans, and Jews, but few Italians and Slavs and very few blacks. Law enforcement, like crime, was an ethnic affair in the big city.

The unusual prominence Italians achieved in the upper reaches of crime resulted from an effective combination of traditional and modern values. The vast majority of the Italians were honest people, to be sure. However, their disorganized communities were marked by poverty, bad living conditions, and a pervasive aura of superstition, hostility toward strangers, a fatalistic attitude toward death and violence, and a nonco-operative spirit toward police and toward modernist laws like Prohibition. The Italian milieu proved conducive to the operations of bootleggers and gangsters. The intensely family-centered particularism of the Italian community facilitated recruitment of kin-folk into large-scale criminal operations, known to outsiders as "the Mafia."

The criminal syndicates grew large and powerful because they mirrored the modern, efficient organizational style of legitimate business enterprises. The territories of neighborhood gangs were enlarged to include whole sectors of Chicago, and soon to sophisticated countywide and even national networks, which facilitated recruitment of new members and political payoffs, and provided a large market for illicit services. Criminal activities expanded from petty crime and personal violence (especially kidnapping and extortion) to the control of major industries—illegal liquor traffic, prostitution, gambling (based on elaborate racetrack information services), loan shark practices, and racketeer penetration into legitimate areas such as labor unions, laundries, trucking, and theaters. Like unscrupulous businessmen, the criminal syndicates developed political power (Capone took credit for Thompson's election as mayor of Chicago in 1927), made arrangements with judges and prosecutors and practiced community benevolence, Robin Hood style. They even acquired a touch of high society glamour, as evidenced by press and movie publicity, and garish (and frequent) funerals.

The Italian underworld never was able to make its empire permanent. Recruitment of gang members, based on kinship rather than talent, was inefficient. Advancement in crime depended on skill, of course, but also required avoiding assassination. By 1978, more than 1,000 crime figures in Chicago had been murdered in gangland style. The system was regulated by force, rather than by bureaucratic rules, so eventually personal survival counted more than profit. When the depression came and Prohibition ended, the financial rewards to syndicated crime could no longer support the elaborate infrastructure of expensive bodyguards, skilled lawyers, fancy women, fast cars, and constant payoffs. The industry went into decline rapidly. Furthermore, crime was always illegal. This mattered little when city, county, and state law officers were in alliance with the syndicate. But when honest federal officials entered the scene, or hostile politicians came to power, the corrupt empire crumbled. Capone himself was prosecuted by the federal courts for income tax evasion and locked away in Alcatraz. Throughout Illinois, periodic closing of red light districts, and federal and state prosecution of gamblers eroded the power and plunder of organized crime until narcotics prohibition in the postwar era brought new markets and new profits to a sick industry.

In the segregated black communities of Illinois, criminals always flourished. Nickle-and-dime gambling on the numbers, in the form of the policy wheel, became the largest industry in the black ghetto, affording more employment, more entertainment, and more hope for success in a fatalistic world than anything except its arch rival, the Baptist church. The policy wheels, incidentally, were organized in about as sophisticated a fashion as the Illinois State Lottery, which began in 1974. Prostitution, furthermore, brought white money into the otherwise segregated black community, and provided plenty of jobs for the girls, madams, pimps, maids, caterers, and jazz musicians. Apart from ineffective periodic crackdowns, the white community tolerated prostitution and gambling in the ghetto, so long as the police and sheriff's office received periodic kickbacks and payoffs. The loose family structure of the black underworld inhibited the development of powerful syndicates. In the 1960s, however, a suddenly enlarged market for heroin and other drugs provided new avenues for big money, and the historic vigor of the black underground provided a basis for successful competition with Italian and Hispanic drug dealers.

The unquenchable demand for liquor, prostitution, gambling, and other illicit entertainment guaranteed that Chicago, East Saint Louis, Springfield, and Moline would spawn organized crime. The state's political system tolerated vice because traditionalist politicians needed the votes, money, and patronage that criminal alliances could provide. Middle-class moralists, though always upset, were rarely able to mobilize their forces often enough to raise the cost of vice to prohibitive levels. It is not true, despite frequent stories to the contrary, that the middle classes frequently patronized vice resorts. The middle classes rarely bought illegal liquor or gambled on the numbers or ponies or visited prostitutes. The great majority of clients were always traditional working-class men, either bachelors with cash or husbands with passive wives who meekly accepted the double standard of morality. The working classes rarely joined reform crusades. The middle classes were too often cynical about the hopelessness of reform or too concerned with high taxes to spend the energy needed to fuel successful crusades more than once every four or five years. Perhaps, too, the complex social mix in urban Illinois contributed to a high tolerance of illegal activities so long as they were reasonably secret and did not directly threaten the security of peaceful suburban neighborhoods. Thus it has always been easier to rouse public support for crackdowns on street crimes than on prostitution or gambling. Since most organized crime took place in central cities, suburbanites and rural folk could ignore the existence of vice, and in any case, would have little power to counter it directly.

On the Fourth of July 1929, Illinois orators could wax eloquent about their state. The economy had never been so prosperous. Industry, commerce, real estate, and services flourished. Agriculture had recovered from its postwar slump and farmers were eagerly acquiring electric lights, automobiles, tractors, and household conveniences. Coal mining, it is true, was suffering from low demand. But on the whole, the nearly eight million people who made their homes in the prairie state were optimistic about the future. Society seemed to be improving annually. The schools had become attractive to everyone; churches were smugly proud of their godliness; less poverty was visible than ever before. The one huge embarrassment to modern sensibilities was the blatant crime and political corruption in the larger cities. Even here there was hope, for the political power of criminal syndicates had been broken in Chicago in the 1928 elections. The new president, Herbert Hoover, was determined to maintain prosperity, eliminate poverty in America, and enforce Prohibition by destroying the Al Capones and other bootleggers. The modern ethic which Hoover so well represented seemed on the verge of final triumph in Illinois.

5

Depression and War:
Traditionalism Resurgent

*T*HE buoyant optimism of the early twentieth century reflected the expectation that economic and individual modernization would continue forever, solving all problems one after another until some sort of utopia was achieved. This faith in the future never totally died out in Illinois, but it did fall into disrepute in the 1930s when a nationwide economic crisis dragged the state into a decade-long depression. Unemployment, bankruptcy, and destitution were severe enough in the state; even worse was the psychological depression born of personal worries and the haunting fear that prosperity might never return. Just as Illinoisans realized that national forces had caused the disaster, so too the state discovered that it could neither recover by itself, nor even take care of its own distress without federal help. To a far greater extent than ever before, policies set in Washington and monies appropriated there shaped the texture of private and public life in Illinois. Power and prestige slipped away from the paneled offices of the modernizers to the typewriters of faceless bureaucrats and to the mimeograph machines and bullhorns of the new labor unions. The depression marked a crisis in values and a permanent shift in power everywhere. The Illinois scene was a microcosm of the national story.

The optimism of the modernizers in the 1920s expressed itself in a remarkable building boom. Dozens of new skyscrapers in the Loop testified to a confidence that perpetual prosperity would channel the wealth of the Midwest to the talented managers, bankers, brokers, lawyers, and entrepreneurs of Chicago. New factories went up in every city; steel, meat, machinery, telephones, boxcars, and chemicals could hardly be produced fast enough to meet surging demand. Neighborhood "ma and pa" groceries and dry goods stores gave way to large, efficient chain stores with lower prices and greater variety. Utility companies stretched their telephone, power, and gas lines across every city and town in Illinois. Cities, counties, and the state, especially, borrowed money to pave roads and build highways to handle the cars, buses, and trucks that carried the increased commerce and enlivened movement of people. Banks, insurance houses, and savings and loan companies lent hundreds of millions of dollars for commercial construction and family housing. Sluggish growth in a few sectors, like coal mining, was shrugged off as an aberration in the new era of prosperity.

While state and national leaders talked about eventually ending poverty through sustained economic growth, the modernized middle class enjoyed the tangible fruits of progress. Chicago advertising agencies—smaller than New York's but equally effective—taught consumers how to enjoy their wealth by buying handsomely designed automobiles, houses, appliances, furniture, and clothes. Families with a reliable income but little savings were told they need not wait for the better things in life. Installment purchases, credit plans, and long-term housing mortgages became widespread. The modernizers' faith in the future was thereby linked to their search for material fulfillment. Radio, motion pictures, sports extravaganzas, and amusement parks provided commercialized entertainment, while the enormous increase in automobile ownership among the middle class provided the mobility to enjoy the fun.

The prosperity of the 1920s was not a false front to a rotten system. The economy was basically sound, and Illinois was not excessively optimistic. Worker productivity on the farm, in shops, stores, factories, and offices increased steadily. Wages and salaries climbed, as did profits, especially, while inflation remained near zero. The modernization of management practices begun about 1900 promised a continuous rise in productivity. College-educated executives applied new scientific criteria to hiring, training, and promotion practices, ensuring that workers were assigned to appropriate jobs more on the basis of skill than personal connection with foremen. Illinois high schools produced men and women with a knowledge of typing, shorthand, drafting, machine work, and accounting skills, permitting industry to use more efficient, more complex production techniques and office routines. The widespread adoption of pensions, paid vacations, group insurance, incentive systems, and cleaner, safer, more interesting work environments increased employee satisfaction, reduced labor turnover, and enhanced productivity. Careful inventory control and centralized planning encouraged the growth of chains of department, drug, grocery, and even cigar stores, while franchised automobile dealerships and service stations provided uniform services of higher quality than ever dreamed of in the nineteenth century. Everyone in Illinois discovered he or she could work shorter hours, produce more, earn more, and spend more.

How, then, could America have sunk into a severe depression? Superficial analysis blamed the stock market crash of 1929, mistaking one of the first effects for the underlying cause. True, a relatively small number of investors "lost" money in 1929, but mostly that was paper profit created by a temporary surge in stock market prices. President Hoover blamed foreign factors, especially Europe's slow recovery from the world war, conveniently overlooking the fact that the worldwide depression of the 1930s began in the United States, then spread abroad. Franklin Roosevelt pointed his finger at corrupt bankers and speculators and made sure his Justice Department prosecuted Samuel Insull as the number one villain; yet Insull was acquitted in court, and the real mistake of the bankers had been to share the optimism of the entire society. Leftist economists in the 1930s and 1940s blamed the unequal distribution of wealth, arguing that the poor were unable to buy enough to keep the system going. Yet the rapid growth of the middle classes meant that inequality was less in the 1920s than in the previous half-century—and the equality of poverty which characterized the 1930s did nothing to restore prosperity. More recently Chicago economist Milton Friedman has argued that a minor recession in

1929–1930 was transformed into a full-scale depression by the misguided monetary policies of the federal government, which contracted the money supply by a third between 1929 and 1932, forcing banks to cut back sharply on the loans they were providing to keep the system moving.

If historians and economists still dispute the technical causes of the depression, there is little doubt about its genuine severity. The economy began a gradual downward glide in the late summer of 1929, and save for a few false upswings, sank slowly to a nadir in February 1933, touching bottom just as President Roosevelt was inaugurated. The relentless downward spiral sucked in the various sectors of the Illinois economy at different times. First hit were the speculative stock, bond, and commodity markets, real estate, and agriculture. Then came banking, construction, coal mining, heavy industry, and railroads. Education, medicine, and the important wholesale and retail sectors limped through a bad decade, though escaping major disasters. The only growth industry was government, where employment rose and real pay rates actually went up.

The frightening mechanics of contraction droned on relentlessly. With business confidence shattered, bankers scurried to call in doubtful loans, refusing renewals to old customers and scornfully turning away men who thought they had a chance to start a business. Construction of new homes, offices, and factories halted. Prices fell, as did wages, salaries, and rents. Consumers postponed the purchase of automobiles, appliances, furniture, and the like, hoarding their remaining cash for a little longer. Naturally, the drop in demand simply touched off another round of cutbacks, layoffs, bankruptcies, and foreclosures.

The impact of the hard times was worst in communities that depended on mining or heavy manufacturing. Coal mining, an important industry in a dozen central and southern counties, reduced employment by half, with only six months' work a year available for the active miners. The collapse of the agricultural implements and steel markets hit the Quad Cities and South Chicago severely. Taking 1925–1927 average payrolls as 100 percent, by the low point in 1932, factory payrolls plunged to 42 percent in Aurora, 27 percent in Danville, 37 percent in

Decatur, 46 percent in East Saint Louis, 14 percent in Joliet, 47 percent in Peoria, 30 percent in Quincy, 20 percent in Rock Island, 24 percent in Rockford, and a sickening 7 percent of normal in Moline. Chicago payrolls were down to 29 percent, and statewide the low point was also 29 percent. Total factory employment did not fall as far as cash payrolls, since workers were on much-reduced pay scales and short hours; at the nadir, factories employed 52 percent of their normal work force. The rusting of unused equipment was far less a problem than the loss of desperately needed output and wages, and the wasting away of skills. The state's leading railroad, the Illinois Central, saw its revenues cut in half by the depression. Coal, steel, meat, grain, cotton, and merchandise were not in demand, and passenger service fell off dramatically as businessmen, tourists, and paying migrants stayed home. The Illinois Central responded by firing more than half of its 60,000 employees, curtailing service, postponing maintenance and new equipment purchases, cutting wages 10 percent, and suspending dividends to stockholders. The fixed burden of interest on bonds could not be reduced, however, and the Illinois Central verged on bankruptcy until $11 million in federal loans saved the system. Even so, Illinois Central stock fell from $137 in 1930 to a mere $5 per share in 1932, and dividends were not resumed until 1950.

Memories of losing the savings of a lifetime haunted the survivors of the decade. Few, however, were ruined by bank failures. Hundreds of small downstate banks and little institutions in the Chicago neighborhoods went bankrupt, especially in the summer of 1932 and in the aftermath of Roosevelt's bank holiday in 1933. Most of the depositors had already withdrawn their savings, and the rest were eventually paid off at an average rate of eighty cents or ninety cents on the dollar, after long months or even years of anxiety. The bank owners usually lost every cent they had. The people who lost their life savings were some of the capitalists, on the one hand, and the unemployed who had to spend their assets to survive, on the other.

The resilience and ingenuity of the people were sorely tested by the depression. Half the families in Illinois had to endure shorter or longer stretches of unemployment at one time or another during the decade. In the coal camps and in Chicago's black belt, most families were unemployed most of the time, while at the other extreme farmers were seldom without work. Even where unemployment did not strike it remained a threat, and it hit relatives, friends, and neighbors who sought to "borrow" food, old clothes, discarded toys, and a little hard cash. Families on reduced incomes economized drastically. Telephones were disconnected, all major purchases postponed, travel plans cancelled. Backyard gardens sprang up around the state, and home canning changed from a pastime to a necessity. Young couples put off marriage; older ones postponed their third or fourth child, and so the birth rate fell to zero growth levels. Reliance on soups and potatoes stretched food budgets, while the pressure cooker made tough cuts of meat as palatable as their price. Clothes, cars, and appliances were patched and repaired and taped together to last a little longer. Candy again became a "treat." Churches and lodges redistributed clothes, furniture, and food baskets among their members, and public health officials nervously watched for signs that declining nutritional standards might be producing more ill health. Death rates, however, continued to drop as medical science combatted infectious diseases. By 1932 many families had doubled up with relatives, and others were skipping rent or mortgage payments. In Peoria, which weathered the decade better than other cities, 22 percent of the rents were delinquent in 1933, since the average income of tenants had fallen by a third since 1929. Landlords were reluctant to evict, because the legal procedure cost money, the debt would never be repaid, and the likelihood of finding a new paying tenant was bleak. Thousands of kindhearted landlords in Illinois lost their buildings because they could not collect their rents—a lot of mean landlords went broke, too. Three out of eight home mortgages in Peoria were in arrears by 1933—but half the homeowners had deeds to their property free and clear, and banks were likewise reluctant to foreclose.

The psychological impact of unemployment was devastating. Men who had absorbed modern values blamed themselves for their failure to find adequate work. In working-class homes the inability of the husband to fulfill his basic duty of protecting and feeding his family brought humiliation. Women reluctantly became acting heads of families, as they economized on spending and provided what leadership there was. Girls growing up in deprived families acquired responsibilities fast, and after the Second World War showed a striking interest in becoming homemakers and mothers, this time in an era of affluence. Relatives and neighbors drew closer together in a spirit of shared hardship. Yet the truism that economic worries are the basis for marital discord was not repealed. Frustration gave way to arguments; men deserted their families; tens of thousands of boys— and some girls—left home, only to wander the land aimlessly as tramps and hoboes. Self-confidence, faith in the future, hopes for advancement—core values of the modernizers—became victims of the failure of the modern economy to meet the needs of the people.

In normal times Illinois could take care of its destitute through township relief and private charity. Help was available for orphans, sick, elderly, and other people clearly unable to survive in a modern economy geared for the benefit of men with jobs. In 1929 and 1930 strenuous efforts were made to relieve distress through the old system. If a family had exhausted its savings, cashed in its life insurance, sold its house and car, then the community chest or township officials would conduct an investigation and furnish a food requisition good for flour, powdered milk, vegetables, and a little meat at co-operating grocery stores. The system was utterly unsuited to a crisis of the magnitude of the depression. It broke down totally in the coal region, where the national Red Cross had to intervene, setting up soup kitchens to prevent starvation. Landlords, on the verge of bankruptcy themselves, tore down the coal miners' shabby houses to escape property taxes. By 1932 Chicago, Rock Island, and Moline had run out of public relief funds. The private agencies, after doubling and quadrupling their budgets in 1930 and 1931 until contributions began falling off, were totally swamped by urgent pleas for help. The township governments across the state likewise expanded their aid until falling tax revenues undercut their efforts in 1932.

At last Springfield acted. A bond issue provided funds for Chicago and other hard-hit areas. Stepped-up construction expenditures and a reduction of property taxes by 20 percent helped a little, but the state's fiscal system was unable to cope with the crisis. The state supreme court struck down an income tax as unconstitutional under the old 1870 state constitution. Federal help was needed desperately but, apart from a few small loans, was not forthcoming because the political stalemate in Washington had paralyzed the federal government. Illinois was helpless, and the National Guard began monthly reports to the governor on the threat of violence around the state.

In chronicling the hardships of the depression years it must be recalled that Illinois remained basically rich. The farm lands and mines were unscathed; the advantages that accrued to the state as the hub of the national rail, trucking, and inland waterway transportation systems continued; the millions of sturdy homes, the shops, stores, factories, and skyscrapers remained standing. The talents and skills of the people stood as high as ever, if only they could be organized and brought to bear on the need for food, shelter, and services. Illinois had everything needed for prosperity, yet, eerily, an unmade, unnatural human disaster had occurred. Men who still possessed wealth gathered in their clubs to ponder the histories of other lands, whispering the fearful questions: Would there be a revolution? Would rioting mobs seize power in the streets? Could anything be done?

Violence did occur in Illinois but not in the city streets. The gangsters in Chicago were still shooting each other, though with the arrest of Al Capone in 1931, the legalization of beer and liquor in 1933, and the Chicago crackdown on gambling that same year the awful decade of rampant syndicate crime was ending. Violence was endemic in the coal fields, however, as rival miners' unions used their knowledge of dynamite to blast each other into oblivion. The coal miners were the only legitimate organized group in the state with the resources in manpower, nerve, discipline, and socialist ideology to launch a radical attack on capitalism. But a full-scale war between the national union leadership and Illinois socialist miners drained their energy and made them ciphers in the political upheavals of the early 1930s.

Except in Granite City, where distress was acute, the National Guard discovered very little talk of revolution in Illinois. Farmers were following with disdain the sporadic agrarian violence in western Iowa. There was no real trouble in rural Illinois, though in Will County angry farmers attended foreclosure sales and saved a friend's property by bidding a few dollars for it, scaring away other bidders, then returning it to him. In Rock Island, however, the middle class was especially bitter in early 1933, for all the banks had shut down, normal business was at a standstill, and no one could get at his savings. In several cities "unemployed councils" held sparsely attended rallies. The National Guard attributed the councils to agitators from Chicago. In Chicago (where the blame was shifted to Reds from New York), Communists held rallies demanding more relief, and in a few cases forcibly stopped evictions. More serious in the metropolis was a taxpayers' strike, which brought the city to the edge of bankruptcy. The Chicago school teachers were paid with script that sold at a heavy discount, but at least they had guaranteed jobs. The mood of Illinois in the winter of 1932–1933 was not revolt or panic, but disbelief, incomprehension, despair, and above all, loss of faith in the promise of modernization.

Illinois was helpless in the winter of 1932–1933. With its economy inextricably tied to national and international markets, nothing the people of the state could do would reverse the downward slide toward total economic collapse. The political stalemate in Washington meant that the federal government was itself paralyzed until Franklin Roosevelt's inauguration. Illinois waited helplessly as more banks and businesses closed, as unemployment engulfed a fourth of the labor force, as relief funds gave out and local government verged on bankruptcy. No one knew if the new Democratic administration would be able to provide relief for the desperately needy, recovery for the shattered economy, or long-term reform to prevent a recurrence of the tragedy. Everyone realized that federal action was the last hope to save the modernized society that had been built in Illinois and America, so there was near unanimous support, at first, for anything Roosevelt would do.

The first task of the New Deal was to restore confidence in America's future. "We have nothing to fear but fear itself," President Roosevelt declared in his first address. Dramatic actions followed immediately, cumulating in radical changes in the way the economy operated, in the treatment of the poor, and in the political alignments in the country. There were so many programs and new departures involved in the alphabetical agencies of the New Deal that it would take a whole book to cover them all. Some major programs, such as the Tennessee Valley Authority and the efforts to help distressed cotton farmers, did not affect Illinois directly—though their repercussions, such as the northward migration of millions of displaced black farmers, had a delayed impact on life in the state years, even decades afterwards. The New Deal represented an immense intrusion of federal power into private and public affairs in Illinois. It was comparable to the effect of war, except the changes were far more deliberate and permanent. The diversity of Illinois made the experience in one state a microcosm of the effects everywhere.

Roosevelt's first move was to close all the banks in the country and then allow only the soundest to reopen. The losses that resulted were immense; probably the situation had deteriorated so much that no other course was possible. Roosevelt himself had a strong traditionalist bent. He was suspicious of Wall Street and LaSalle Street bankers, blaming them for the speculative rampage of the 1920s that he thought had caused the depression. New controls on the securities industry, and a systematic federal effort to break up the electrical utility holding companies and to jail Chicago's leading entrepreneur, Samuel Insull, emphasized Roosevelt's distrust of modernizers and focused popular resentment. Hatred of the bankers for misdirecting the economy would become a major weapon in political realignment. The president was so hostile to the moneychangers that he even opposed federal bank deposit insurance, seeing it as a device to allow corrupt bankers to avoid responsibility for their sins.

The modernist ideals of efficiency and continuously improving management held little charm for most New Dealers. They diagnosed the trouble with the economy as excessively low prices and purchasing power, and worked valiantly to raise wages and farm prices, to exclude low-paid children and women from the labor force, to suspend laissez-faire competition among businessmen, and to build up the power of labor unions and farmers. At the same time, emergency financial help would go to prevent mortgages from being foreclosed on homes, farms, and railroads. Economic planning was shifted out of the supposedly irresponsible grasp of modernizing businessmen in favor of new federal agencies that, ideally, recognized that the era of rapid economic growth had ended, and the services of hustling entrepreneurs were no longer needed in America. Roosevelt could laugh off the hatred he earned in the boardrooms of Chicago and Peoria and in the posh country clubs because the New Deal had captured popular favor with its vigor, determination, and easy identification of villains.

Regardless of upper-class hatred of Roosevelt, the New Deal did help business survive the depression. New federal funds and guaranties shored up the financial system and the railroads. Immense spending programs—financed by borrowing that doubled the national debt—pumped hundreds of millions of dollars into the economy, allowing the recipients to pay off debts, buy food and clothing, and give something to the landlord. Until the natural productive forces in the economy could recover, federal spending was essential in restoring demand for goods and services, allowing small manufacturers and subcontractors to reopen their shops, storekeepers to stock new lines of goods, and landlords to pay their gas bills. The recovery of the mid-1930s, so far as it went, benefitted chiefly the businessmen, the middle classes, and skilled blue-collar workers. Recovery was not complete enough to help the poor, blacks, the aged, or the young who were without jobs.

Most of the federal spending went where it was most desperately needed, in the form of relief payments to unemployed families. At first, relief came in the form of the dole—that is, cash payments for which no work was required. Although this was the most efficient mode of helping the distressed, it violated one of the most basic modern values, that income ought to be linked to productivity. The modernizing ethic placed an ugly stigma on idle, able-bodied men, especially those who receive handouts. Acceptance of a dole was widely seen as a sign of moral failure, of a lack of foresight, ability, and ambition. Middle-class men on relief felt especially humiliated. Furthermore, it was an insult to the taxpayer, himself hard pressed in the 1930s. Thousands of people eligible for relief payments because of their reduced incomes refused to undergo the embarrassment of a means test. Most of those who did accept relief were unable to shake off the feeling that they were somehow guilty, or personally responsible, for the failure of the economy. Springfield agreed with Washington that a modern society could not long tolerate a massive dole. Governor Horner often warned of the "constant danger" of establishing a "pauper class" in Illinois. He confided to a friend that the dole "is bound to be enervating to what we have been proud to call American vitality and courage." The head of Sears, Roebuck, allowing that "it is probably true that we cannot allow everyone to starve (although I personally disagree with this philosophy)," insisted that "we should tighten up relief all along the line, and if relief is to be given it must be on a bare subsistence allowance."

Washington decided what relief policy was to be, and it emphasized make-work projects. The Civilian Conservation Corps took a hundred thousand unemployable young men, ages seventeen to twenty-three, off the streets of Chicago, Danville, and Alton, shipped them for six months to out-of-state rural work camps, and sent $22 of each $30 monthly wage to the boys' families. There was no comparable program for young women. Vastly larger in size was the Works Progress Administration, which between 1935 and 1940 employed upward of 200,000 Illinois men at any one time, and more than 1,000,000 altogether. In 1938, at its peak, the WPA in Illinois had a larger work force than General Motors and Chrysler, combined, had nationwide.

Although a means test was necessary to get a WPA job, the worker no longer had to consult a social worker to explain how he was spending his money. Roosevelt had envisioned the WPA as a way of conserving the talents of unemployed men, though in fact most of the jobs created required very little skill. Ex-machinists became timekeepers, plumbers shovelled gravel, trained lawyers clipped newspapers. Pay scales were kept just above subsistence levels, so that no one would refuse a "real" job if it became available. Supervision was mediocre, and most of the men were below average in work habits to begin with, so the waste was considerable if judged by industry's standards of efficiency. But the WPA was basically a relief program, and it left the state a valuable legacy in the form of roads, bridges, sewers, sidewalks, school buildings, playgrounds, and airports. Few men recalled their WPA days with pride; their families were more appreciative. The daughter of a downstate Croatian blacksmith remembered well that day in 1935 when her father was transferred from the dole to a WPA project. "This was a godsend. It meant food, you know. Survival, just survival." She also remembered her nursing school classmate, the daughter of a physician, who ridiculed these "lazy" people, these "shovel leaners." She fumed, finally shouting back that it was "just like the patients we take care of. None of them are in that hospital by choice!" After calming down she reflected, "Gee, these are just two separate, separate worlds."

Between 1929 and 1942, about half the people in Illinois received government relief, in one form or another at one time or another. At any one time, no more than 20 percent received relief, but turnover on the rolls was high. A semiskilled or unskilled factory, construction, service, or farm laborer was four or five times more likely to have received relief than a white-collar worker, and he was on relief longer, and returned often. Probably 75 to 85 percent of the blue-collar work force (they outnumbered the white-collar workers) were eventually on relief, versus perhaps 20 to 25 percent of the white-collar workers. Although exact data is lacking, it seems likely that nearly all the blacks in the state received relief, at least intermittently. Despite the vast effort, at any one time a third to a half of the people in Illinois who needed help were not getting it, simply because there was never enough money to go around.

By the late 1930s unemployment continued to hover at 15 percent of the labor force, but disaster had been averted. The New Deal had saved the corporations and banks and railroads from total collapse, and the unemployed from starvation. The federal government had turned relief of the unemployable back to the states, which required Illinois to levy a painful 3 percent sales tax. New joint state-federal programs provided old age assistance, unemployment insurance, and aid to dependent children and promised that the employed would eventually receive social security pensions. These permanent cushions guaranteed that future economic reversals would not repeat the hardships of the early 1930s, but they did not rescue the economy from stagnation; full recovery was not in sight.

Agriculture in Illinois suffered severely in the earlier part of the depression, particularly 1931 and 1932. The farmers' prosperity had lagged behind that of urbanites in the 1920s; now their distress helped pull the rest of the state's economy down. The chief problem was simply a fall in demand for beef, milk, and pork, which caused a severe drop in both animal and grain prices. The average receipts of Illinois farmers fell 60 percent between the late 1920s and the early 1930s. Since expenses dropped at about the same rate as income (except taxes, which increased), the farmers seldom were forced into bankruptcy. Both Hoover and Roosevelt set up programs to provide emergency refinancing of farm mortgages, to prevent a repetition of the financial crisis that smashed farmers immediately after the First World War. In the 1920s the average Illinois farm represented a $25,000 investment in land—half were owned by the operator, and otherwise by absentee landlords. Another $10,000 per farm represented machinery, livestock, inventories, and other assets owned by the farm operator or tenant. Therefore, the farmer, whether owner or tenant, was a relatively wealthy man even though his assets in 1935 were only half those of 1925. His assets may have been immobile, but seldom did he have to worry about going on relief. However, unskilled farm laborers frequently lost their jobs and swelled the rural relief rolls as farmers cut expenses. Farmers also economized by postponing the purchase of new tractors, trucks, and implements. This, of course, further depressed the state's huge agricultural machinery industry.

The Roosevelt administration had a traditionalist affection for agriculture. The president himself grossly exaggerated its importance; he idolized the Jeffersonian image of the sturdy yeoman farmer uncorrupted by the vices of the metropolis. Consequently the New Deal sponsored a number of programs to enhance the incomes, security, and quality of life on the family farm. The Rural Electrification Administration, for example, helped increase the number of Illinois farmsteads lighted by electricity from 16 percent in 1930 to 43 percent in 1940. It was unable to stem the retreat of telephones, from 69 percent in 1930 to 52 percent in 1940, for here was a luxury that could easily be removed. The major New Deal farm program tried to raise farm incomes by cutting back production, which would raise prices. This technique worked well for the cotton and wheat belts, but proved wholly unsuccessful for the diversified corn-hog-dairy situation in Illinois. However, severe drought in 1934 and again in 1936 did raise prices. Paradoxically, drought, destruction, and higher prices meant major gains to the commercial farmer, at the expense, of course, of the consumer. Even after the price rise, city dwellers were paying a third less for their food in the 1930s than in the 1920s.

After the Supreme Court declared the first federal farm program unconstitutional, the Congress legislated another one, whose philosophy dominated federal farm policies until the new food scarcity of the 1970s. The policy, largely developed by wealthy corn-belt farmers in the Farm Bureau Federation, moved away from the use of federal moneys as a mode of relief for poor and marginal farmers. The idea was to stabilize the production and prices of major crops (and thus, indirectly, of cattle and hogs) by setting acreage allotments under the guise of land conservation policy. Roosevelt bought the idea because he was enamored of saving the topsoil from erosion. Farsighted Illinois farmers liked the plan because it would provide the security they needed for making a final, all-out effort to make agriculture totally modern. Agribusiness, rather than the subsistence family farm, would be the ideal. The policy was a stunning success for the survivors, who bought up neighboring farms and invested heavily in new machinery and biotechnology. By the 1970s, Illinois farmers had average assets in hundreds of thousands of dollars. The marginal farmers, especially those in southern Illinois, were not helped at all. They could only drift to the cities.

The political repercussions of the depression lasted for decades. The first, most dramatic result was the collapse in Republican fortunes. The Democrats had long been the minority party in the state, unable before the 1930s to erase the image of the GOP as the force of prosperity and modernization. The failure of President Hoover's efforts naturally inclined voters toward the opposition. Illinois Democrats capitalized on their opportunity, not merely by promising recovery (which they had great difficulty securing), but more importantly by identifying the GOP as callous to the sufferings of the working class. Longstanding rhetoric to the effect that the GOP was the tool of bankers, industrialists, and speculators suddenly struck home as millions blamed the economic elite for the sad fate of the society.

To solidify their advantages into a permanent standing majority the Democrats had to mobilize the discontent of the working classes. This became possible with the government-sponsored rise of aggressive labor unions in the mid-1930s. The coal miners, finally settling their bitter civil war, moved to organize the unskilled labor forces in the great meatpacking, steel, clothing, and machinery industries of Chicago, East Saint Louis, and Rock Island–Moline. In contrast to the bloody battles in other states, notably Michigan and Pennsylvania, the Illinois effort was relatively peaceful. Only one serious violent confrontation occurred, when Chicago police opened fire on peaceful demonstrators at the Republic steel plant on Memorial Day 1937. The coal miners, with help from the garment unions, organized unskilled ethnic workers into a militant, intensely pro-Roosevelt CIO. The older crafts unions of the AF of L, challenged by the aggressive CIO, responded with their own large-scale organizing drives. They signed up even larger numbers of workers, particularly in trucking and building trades, and in the stockyards.

By the end of the decade, a fourth of the state's industrial labor force was aligned with the AF of L or the CIO. During the war years, further major gains came among steel, electrical, automobile, and machinery workers. With a few exceptions (like the Chicago public school teachers), unions were unable to attract white-collar workers. The pattern of class differentiation was sharply set: most blue-collar workers were avid union members, most white-collar workers rejected the concept. Undoubtedly the unemployment and relief experiences of the two classes determined this sharp split. Blue-collar workers had suffered much more severely and were desperate for security. The unions promised not only higher wages, but far more importantly, more job security. The arbitrary power of foremen to fire or humiliate a man at whim was always the first grievance union contracts eliminated. Although union leaders realized that business conditions determined the size of the work force, and that layoffs were inevitable from time to time, they found an ideal way to protect their best members: seniority. By reducing the power of the foremen, resisting efforts of management to control closely the speed of work, and installing a seniority system for automatic movements to better jobs, the unions eliminated much of the capriciousness, uncertainty, and insecurity of blue-collar jobs. By taking credit for wage increases, pension plans, fringe benefits, and protective legislation in Washington and Springfield, unions secured the strong loyalty of their rank and file. By throwing their financial and manpower reserves into election campaigns, typically behind Democratic candidates, the unions gained political power. Henceforth, governors, legislators, mayors, and city councils would listen when organized labor took a stand on policy questions. Actually, the unions asked state and local government for little beyond recognition and assurances that union-busting tactics would not be tolerated. Their major policy interest lay at the federal level. Franklin Roosevelt and Harry Truman, realizing that their victories in 1940, 1944, and 1948 depended chiefly on union votes, listened closely.

In 1932, the class division of the popular vote was slight— about 50 percent of the middle class and 60 percent of the working class voted for Roosevelt, both groups having lost confidence in Hoover and the Republicans. By 1936, however, sharp class differences had appeared in Illinois. The Democrats made a systematic appeal to the traditionalism of the poorly educated, insecure, blue-collar workers. The New Deal was openly aligned against the selfish rich, the reckless bankers, the irresponsible industrialists—the foolish modernists who did not understand that their day was over. The country was built up, and the equitable redistribution of wealth and power was now the order of the day. Roosevelt and his running mates ran up fabulous majorities—80 percent of reliefers and WPA workers, 85 percent of CIO members, 80 percent of AF of L members, 72 percent of nonunion blue-collar workers. By judicious use of patronage, in addition to an appeal to traditionalist values (the repeal of Prohibition, for example), Democrats swept 80

percent of the Catholic and 79 percent of the Jewish vote. Most
of the ethnics in Illinois wore blue collars and carried union
cards. Often they had neglected to vote in duller past elections,
especially working-class women who thought politics was a
male affair. Now they turned out in record numbers, as 82 percent of the state's eligible voters went to the polls in 1936,
versus never more than 75 percent in the previous thirty years.
Blacks, bolting Lincoln's party for the first time, switched
en masse to the Democrats, a move whose repercussions would
become dramatic forty years later. The new coalition was heavily urban, as evidenced by Roosevelt's 67 percent in Chicago in
1936, 66 percent in Peoria, and similar margins in Rock Island,
Moline, East Saint Louis, Decatur, and Quincy.

Of course, 1936 was a dismal year for the Republicans all
around. In Illinois they barely carried a majority of the relatively wealthy businessmen, professionals, and farmowners. For
the first time they failed to carry the ranks of the white-collar
workers. However, the old modernist ethic still carried weight
with key pietistic groups, such as the Methodists, Presbyterians,
Congregationalists, and Swedish Lutherans. The GOP was
beaten badly, but it was not dead. Wealth, education, and status
were still in its corner. Republicans were ready to seize on any
weakness in the New Deal juggernaut.

The Republicans did not have long to wait. Everything went
wrong for Roosevelt in his second term. His congressional majorities vanished after an abortive effort to pack the Supreme
Court. The hallowed modernist ideal of supremacy by constitutional law seemed threatened by the president's heavy-handed
moves. Crying "dictatorship," the opposition, led by the *Chicago Tribune,* questioned the entire justification for New Deal
activism. The angry sit-down strikes of the CIO in neighboring
states frightened businessmen, and a fierce antagonism between
the CIO and AF of L divided the most active proponents of the
New Deal coalition. Meanwhile the Democratic party in Illinois
split. In 1932 Mayor Cermak of Chicago, forging a new Democratic machine led by anti-Irish politicians, had slated a quiet
Jewish judge, Henry Horner, for governor. After Cermak's
death in 1933, the Irish under Mayor Kelly and party boss Patrick Nash reappeared, and tried to dictate Horner's patronage

and policies. Specifically, the Chicago machine wanted legalized gambling to shore up the city's revenues. Horner, an intellectual and a modernist (Lincoln was his hero), resisted furiously. In a series of bitter contests pitting the traditionalist machine versus the incorruptible governor and his modernist, anti-Chicago allies, Horner won. Since Roosevelt had thrown his support behind the Kelly-Nash machine, the rupture struck deeply. It would be replayed in the mid-1970s with Dan Walker following Horner's model in his unsuccessful battle with the Cook County (Daley) machine.

Worst of all for the Democrats, the economy failed to continue upward. Another sharp decline in 1937–1938 proved to the middle classes that the New Deal had failed, and that only by a return to modernist principles and business leadership could full prosperity be restored. The old Republican leadership, speaking through the *Chicago Tribune,* found talented young modernists such as Congressman Everett Dirksen and prosecuting attorney Dwight Green to lead them back to victory. The modern wing of the GOP took over the party completely when blacks, ethnics, and workers switched into the Democratic party, for these elements had formed the base of a traditionalist wing of the GOP centered in Chicago. The voting shift in Chicago spelled the total defeat of the traditionalist wing and the GOP in the city. But no matter, with a renewed emphasis on efficiency, rapid economic growth, clean government, and the security inherent in upward social mobility (rather than in relief and unions), the Republicans fully recouped their losses with new gains from white-collar workers, businessmen, farmers, and suburbanites who opposed high taxes, deficit spending, welfare for the "lazy," and militant unions.

The Republicans were unable to stop Roosevelt's victories in the state in 1940 and 1944, or Truman's in 1948. But they did manage to regain complete control of the state legislature, the congressional delegation, and the governor's mansion (except 1948) for two decades. The cost was the polarization of the electorate along class lines, in addition to the old religious divisions. Thus in 1944, Illinois businessmen, professionals, and farmers were 60 percent Republican, while union members were 72 percent Democratic. Looked at another way, Catholic manual workers ranged from 75 to 85 percent Democratic from 1936 through 1974, while white-collar Protestants were 64 to 70 percent Republican. (A few exceptional years, such as the Republican landslides of 1952, 1956, and 1972, or the Democratic landslide of 1964 shifted the percentages, but left the same pattern.) With traditionalists—Catholics, blacks, blue-collar workers—concentrated in Chicago and the East Saint Louis area, and modernists—middle-class Protestants—concentrated downstate and in the suburbs, the state's politics took on a big city–anticity complexion, even though the basic conflicts stemmed from differences much deeper than those of geography.

The legacy of the depression thus revolved around the search for security. Modernists sought security in upward social mobility, in education, in economic growth, in preparing themselves and their children for the changes they hoped would come about. They considered the banking reforms, which guaranteed their savings and helped business growth, to be the best thing Roosevelt had done. They rejected relief and welfare both as a sign of personal maladjustment and as a signal that government was abandoning its responsibility to promote growth. They became "conservatives" in the sense of rejecting liberal New Deal programs and in insisting on a return to the classic modernist values as the only sound basis of society. Grudgingly tolerant of union activity (for blue-collar workers), they feared the economic disruption caused by strikes, and the threat that politically powerful labor unions, acting through the Democratic party, would seek to control business and agriculture and redistribute their hard-earned personal wealth.

Traditionalists sought security through unions, social security, unemployment insurance, and ethnic pride. Roosevelt, as a great leader who articulated their traditionalist values like no one else ever had, captured their imaginations and made them proud of their values. The city machines had been a great help in securing relief during the dark days, and much was to be forgiven them. As the traditionalist sector grew better educated, however, it increasingly adopted the modernist hostility to corruption. The Cook County Democratic machine responded by eliminating the blatant graft and corruption that had scandalized the world in the 1920s. Not that "big shots" didn't prosper through the machine; rather it was done very quietly, even legally. But most important was the machine's co-operation with unions, business interests, and the federal government to ensure a steady flow of benefits and guarantee a high level of employment. When unemployment would creep upward, Illinois Democrats could cry "Hoover, Hoover" and reap some votes. But when prosperity reigned, as it usually did after 1940, the Democrats had to promise to be businesslike and efficient, in effect, to be indistinguishable from the Republicans who henceforth reflected the dominant modernist values of Illinois.

By the late 1930s the people of Illinois had adjusted their lives and their values to the prospect of permanent depression. Early New Deal hopes that full recovery would be prompt collapsed as the economy suffered a relapse in 1937. Unemployment remained above 10 percent, relief rolls stayed high, profits, salaries, and wages remained low, and bleak prospects continued for business expansion or personal advancement. Families had learned to cope with unemployment, short hours, and sustained uncertainty. They squeezed into smaller apartments or took lodgers and hapless relatives into their homes.

The deepest response to a decade of depression was a more profound appreciation of the need for economic security. Government jobs—in the schools, post office, or police and street departments—symbolized freedom from layoffs, and attracted talent never before or since seen. Farmers accepted federal control of crops, milk and meat production, and conservation practices. Smalltown merchants and professionals, though fiercely hostile to the New Deal's anti-entrepreneurial spirit, accepted the farm programs as vital to the economic stability of their communities. Industrialists, vociferously convinced that the New Deal was stifling the economy, grudgingly accepted labor unions, particularly after the sit-down strikes of 1937 proved the unions could cripple factories by withholding unskilled labor. On the eve of war, the giant factories in Chicago, Peoria, and East Saint Louis—steel, meatpacking, farm equipment—were organized by the militant CIO. In Rockford, however, the smaller size of factories and more truculent attitude of the industrialists stopped unions. Industrialists feared the unions would seize effective control of factory operations, destroying the proper responsibilities of management and undercutting the renewed drive for efficiency.

The mind-racking concern for security understandably led people to try to escape from thinking about their troubles. "Amos and Andy"—a Chicago show—was the big hit on the radio. Lavish musicals and costume dramas attracted the most movie patrons. But the newsreels that separated Shirley Temple from John Wayne were increasingly dominated by the menacing gestures of Adolf Hitler. Searching for complete security in an ever-more-dangerous world, the people relied on the broad ocean, the new neutrality laws, and the building of a powerful navy to keep war far away. As the Roosevelt administration took progressively tougher stands against Naziism, the people of Illinois polarized sharply, bitterly over the proper course of foreign policy.

Illinois knew a little about the disruption and heartbreak engendered by total war. No one wanted the ordeal. Yet everyone in the state recoiled in horror at Hitler's aggression against both Eastern and Western Europe and at the threat Japan posed to the progress of the Far East. Unanimous support greeted Washington's buildup of strong military and naval forces to defend America. The outbreak of war in Europe raised the issue: could America best defend itself from Axis aggression by staying neutral or by aiding Britain and Russia? As the debate played out, rearmament spending brought a return to prosperity. Patriotism was good business. The hard question remained: how could America most effectively—and at lowest cost in American lives—stop Hitler's dictatorship from spreading across the globe, making obscene Lincoln's dream of liberty, Wilson's vision of modernity?

At first, the larger, more articulate side demanded isolationism. Led by industrialists and Republican politicians, the conservative wing of the isolationists warned that another involvement in the old world's tragedies would lead to dictatorship at home, spelling the final demise of both economic and political freedoms. German Americans recoiled at the thought their ordeal of 1917–1918 might be repeated anew. Irish Americans saw no value in saving the British Empire; Scandinavians likewise favored an isolationist policy. Liberal isolationists came to the same conclusions from the opposite directions. Intellectuals, labor leaders, and radicals feared big business would control the war effort, using the false appeal of patriotism to undo the reforms already enacted or tantalizingly close to fruition. Articulate blacks felt the war for democracy and against racism had to be fought inside the United States; Europeans were oppressive colonial powers no matter what their politics; only the Japanese talked about uplifting the colored races.

The interventionists valued security, democracy, and liberty as highly as the isolationists. They, too, saw America as the last refuge of these virtues. But their ideal of the American mission was more active. Unless the United States aided Britain the torch of modern values would be extinguished in Europe by the reactionary Nazis. Arguing, for the most part, that American boys should not do the shooting, the interventionists rallied behind Roosevelt's policy of giving all possible military and economic aid to England short of war. Ethnic groups with relatives in countries overrun by Germany, notably Jews, Czechs, and Poles, stepped up their demands for interventionist policies. They were already Democrats, and Roosevelt's actions further solidified their vote. Although no Samuel Insull emerged as spokesman for British immigrants, the state's influential Episcopalians favored all aid to Britain. Since most Episcopalians (and also Methodists with British grandparents) were Republicans, they found themselves at odds with their party's isolationist tone, shrilly sounded by the *Chicago Tribune*. However, the surprise nomination of Wendell Willkie as the 1940 Republican candidate permitted them to stay in the GOP without an emotional crisis.

Months before Pearl Harbor the isolationists knew their cause was doomed. Roosevelt had apparently succeeded in both building up national defenses and getting vital supplies to Britain without war. Furthermore, even the isolationists supported a hard policy against Japan. Interventionists across the state, angered at the bitter tone of the *Chicago Tribune,* welcomed the appearance of an aggressive, pro-New Deal competitor, Marshall Field's *Chicago Sun*. The first issue of the *Sun* hit the stands on December 4, 1941—to be greeted by the *Tribune's* sensational revelation of the Pentagon's top secret war plans! Three days later Pearl Harbor transformed the *Tribune,* and the remaining isolationists, into fiery war hawks.

Even before Pearl Harbor, sentiment had crystallized to aid Britain at the risk of war. Only persons of German, Italian, and Irish-Catholic descent remained opposed. Scandinavians switched to the interventionist side after the invasion of Norway. Better-educated, wealthier persons, especially those of British or Jewish descent, were most hawkish. By September 1941, the Catholics had finally accepted the interventionist position, spearheaded by Poles and others with relatives in occupied Europe.

The attack on Pearl Harbor instantly galvanized the people into all-out support of the war. No voice was raised against the commitment to total destruction of Japan and Germany. In dramatic contrast to the Mexican War, the Civil War, the Great War of 1917, Korea, and Vietnam, antiwar sentiment was virtually nonexistent. Elijah Muhammed, prophet of the small new Black Muslim sect in Chicago, went to prison for counseling draft evasion, but he was exceptional. The vast majority of Illinois blacks, their numbers swelled by the urgent demands of war production, supported a "double V" campaign: victory over the Axis abroad, and over racial discrimination at home. When rumors filtered through that Hitler had begun destroying European Jews, the Jewish community in the United States did not argue that the policy of unconditional surrender should be changed in an effort to bargain for Jewish lives. (Most people, however, did not learn of the holocaust until 1945.)

Unlike Wilson, Roosevelt did not present the war as a crusade to modernize the world. The basic justifications were traditional: self-defense, the day of infamy as an affront to national honor, the need to destroy totally the Axis to guarantee national security. Propaganda focused on the heinous Japanese, not on the horrors of Nazism (the latter theme came to the fore *after* 1945). Nor did the United States demand a commitment to liberal democracy by its allies—hardly a possibility when the Communist regime of the Soviet Union was taking the brunt of the war effort. Practically the only shred of Wilsonian idealism injected into popular consciousness in the Second World War was a hazy plan for a United Nations.

Illinois escaped the ideological frenzy that had characterized the First World War. Spies were not hunted down everywhere, aliens were not terrorized, German culture was not extirpated. In September 1942, a nervous Lutheran pastor in Randolph County asked the governor to approve his use of German sermons. He had abandoned it when the war began, but his older parishioners had difficulty with English. They were entirely loyal, he explained, adding that thirty-two young men were already in the armed services. The director of war mobilization reassured the pastor that German language sermons were perfectly correct, noting that the man who trained our revolutionary troops was a German who could not speak English.

Repeated reassurances overcame the uneasiness of German Americans, who bought bonds heavily, encouraged their young men to enlist, and refused to support anything resembling antiwar activities. The prewar pro-Nazi "German American Bund" was weak in Illinois; most of its members were young immigrants newly arrived from Germany. The state's large German element was now almost completely assimilated. Little or no trace of Germanic culture remained in Illinois.

When Japanese Americans were removed from the Pacific Coast, the army resettled 20,000 in Chicago. A few incidents were reported. When four Nisei students were admitted to Elmhurst College, the local American Legion unit complained, but the student body voted overwhelmingly to welcome them. By the end of the war the Japanese were well settled in the city and had been accepted by employers and labor unions. Restrictions on enemy aliens were light, chiefly involving red tape to gain permission to work in war plants. On Columbus Day 1942, Italian aliens (a large proportion of the Italian community) were relieved of "enemy" status. So tolerant were wartime Illinoisans that Italian and German prisoners of war were accepted as farm and arsenal workers and even allowed to fraternize with the Quad Cities girls.

If a crusade for modernity was not apparent in foreign policy, it did provide the ideas Illinois used to organize its war effort.

The people were confident that American know-how would smash the Axis. Carefully planned co-operation between government and the people would triumph over raw terror. The inventive entrepreneurial talents of the modern sector, so long frustrated by depression, were put to their test. Mass production would win victory with fewest casualties. Roosevelt himself recognized that his old enemies were indispensable and were eager to prove their values. Industrialists, bankers, and conservative leaders took over the high posts of the federal government: the war department, the navy (headed by Chicagoan Frank Knox, who enlisted everyone he knew), and notably, the new agencies charged with mobilizing the economy for total war.

The United States fielded 16 million soldiers to fight the war. Illinois, with one million under arms at one time or another, did her share. The selection of these troops required delicate, but urgent, balancing of needs. Equality of sacrifice—an especially modern ideal—was appealed to in order to avoid the political and regional distortions of the Civil War. On the other hand, local control of the selection procedure was a highly valued democratic ideal. Some 561 draft boards across the state, composed of civilian volunteers (usually local elites), balanced national, community, and personal needs. No matter how hungry the military was for manpower, the local boards strenuously resisted drafting fathers until the last year of the war. Illinois did not want, and did not get, many war orphans. The power of agriculture showed, both at the national and the local level, when it secured large numbers of deferments for young farmers and farm laborers on the grounds that food production was a vital war industry. Although 12 percent of the men in the state were farmers, only 4 percent of the soldiers were drawn from agriculture. Because conscientious objectors were few, compared with other wars, society could afford to deal understandingly with them. Men under thirty holding critical jobs in the war industries were usually deferred until the last stages of war. By 1944 the manpower shortages in industry were eased, but the army needed large numbers of soldiers for invasion duty. Rather than dip into the ranks of fathers or older men, the draft boards selected men with occupational deferments, including farmers at last. Had the war lasted longer, or had the people doubted the value of the war, the dilemmas faced by local draft boards might have led to crises like those of the Civil War. As it happened, Illinois produced her share of soldiers without seriously disrupting either the economy or the families of the state, and without moving toward full-scale government control of civilian manpower.

The modernity of the Second World War revealed itself most dramatically in new weapons—the atom bomb, radar, airplanes, proximity fuses, rockets, and the like—and in less obvious, though equally important, developments in medicine, penicillin and antimalaria drugs. The objective in every case was to substitute expensive machinery and advanced science and technology for muscle and blood. Americans were extravagant with money and jealous of lives. Battlefield tactics and general strategy were likewise planned to avoid risk of life by waiting until the Allies had overwhelming force before moving. The result was that only 2 percent of the soldiers were killed in battle, and 4 percent wounded—rates of sacrifice far lower than the gods of war were accustomed to claiming.

Brute force lost to planning, training, and organization. Only one-fourth of the soldiers were assigned combat roles; the others were distributed in equal numbers to clerical, skilled, and semi-skilled operations. Officers were selected not on the basis of social class but on their scores in aptitude tests. For the first time in warfare the military tried to make systematic use of the civilian skills of the men, whether as cooks, truck drivers, accountants, or radio hobbyists. The urgent demands for technical skills to operate a vast, highly mechanized operation led to some frustration. About half the men with needed skills had their square pegs fitted into round holes. The solution—expensive but necessary—to the conflicting demands of proper placement and urgent need was intensive training in the states. Colleges were converted into war-technology institutes. The army taught machinists how to bake meat loaf and telephone repairmen how to direct traffic. The soldiers, their thoughts always focused on postwar life, eagerly snatched the opportunity for learning valuable skills. Aware of the inadequacies of their education in an increasingly technological society, they decided to make a high school or college diploma their first priority once the "damn war" was over.

Illinois soldiers did not, of course, have a unique service record. Indeed their common experiences with men from other states helped homogenize American society and attitudes after the war. Military service mixed people from different states and different backgrounds. Thirty-five states, for example, were represented in a single class of airmen at Scott Field in southern Illinois, and a million bluejackets—one-third of the navy—received basic training and specialized instruction at the Great Lakes Naval Training Station, north of Chicago. Three-fourths of the Illinois men served abroad. Inveterate sightseers, they wrote the folks back home about the splendor of the Vatican, the geraniums in Australia, the quaint villages of France, the jungle life of India. Soldiers stationed in California and Florida began reconsidering their postwar plans with migration in mind. New lands and people impressed some boys as "just like the travelogues in the movies"; but most were only too eager to get back to Main Street or wait for an El train again.

The soldier's personal esprit depended on rank and unit of service. Officers were far more likely to be in good spirits and feel proud of their duties than were enlisted men. Morale was good in the air force and smaller elite units; elsewhere the GIs grumbled about their waste of time and talent, the absurdities of bureaucracy, and the advantages enjoyed by officers and civilians. The men realized they had a job to do, but their sense of war aims was exceedingly dim. Only one man in seven thought in terms of idealistic purposes, like destroying fascism. "I do not mind giving my life for my country and what it stands for—home, Helen, you, free thought, free business, free speech, free religion, and most of all a country free from graft, and it is far from that now," wrote a Montgomery County man to his grandfather (his father had been killed in the First World War). One in twenty was openly cynical: "It is not easy to see one's buddy shot down before one's eyes and then to think of all the blood money made by his death," wrote another Illinois GI.

The manpower problem faced by the country was staggering. From 100 million persons fourteen and over in 1940, by 1944 some 11 million were added to the armed forces, and 7 million were added to civilian employment rolls. Where were these 18 million people (1 million in Illinois) to come from, and how could their transfer be accomplished without a counterproductive disruption of the society? Fortunately, a huge reservoir of unemployed was available: 42 percent of the nation's manpower needs came from a complete reabsorption of this pool. Another 24 percent came from favorable population growth patterns as the baby boom of the late 1920s reached maturity. College and high school enrollment shrank, adding another 17 percent of the new manpower. A significant 14 percent came from housewives who entered the labor force, and the remaining 3 percent came from a shrinkage in the agricultural labor force. As an extra bonus for the war effort, longer hours and overtime added the equivalent of 5 million more workers.

Illinois treated its returning veterans handsomely. They were rapidly reabsorbed by industry (taking places temporarily filled by women). The GI bill enabled a majority of the veterans to attend college or trade school and helped them buy houses in the suburbs at low cost. The state paid out $400 million in bonus money. By 1978 the federal government had paid out a grand total of more than $5 billion dollars to Illinois veterans of the Second World War. That much again, and more, will be spent before the hidden costs of the war are liquidated. Although veterans and their families comprised nearly half the population in the 1970s, and the more affluent half at that, they considered their benefits not as welfare, but as delayed earnings for the unpleasantries of service and the loss of opportunity.

War restored prosperity to Illinois. Meat and grain prices soared, farmers' net income tripled, and land values doubled. Factories reopened with high-priority, cost-plus war contracts. The need for army camps, new plants, and emergency housing revived the construction industry. Main Street and State Street swelled with shoppers. Acute labor shortages developed in manufacturing centers where a few years before the outlook seemed desperate. Unemployment vanished, and tens of thousands of high school youth, old people, and mothers entered the labor force, filling the jobs newly created by the boom or newly vacated by departing soldiers. The index of real per capita income, adjusted for inflation with 1929 as a base of 100, rose from a paltry 61 in 1933 to 89 in 1937, passed 100 in 1941, and peaked at 139 in 1944 (compared with 280 in 1978).

Illinois had three dollars of income in 1944 for every dollar in 1933, but not all could be spent. Four dollars out of ten had to go to the war effort, channelled there by war bonds and heavy new taxes. Strict price controls and coupon book rationing of meat, sugar, gasoline, shoes, and tires prevented a repeat of the runaway inflation of the earlier wars, and ensured that every segment of society would obtain an equitable share of necessities. Major purchases of consumer durables—new housing, automobiles, appliances—became impossible, though the supply of food, clothing, and services remained adequate. The standard of living rose only slightly as the people saved their money, paid old debts, or began to discover withholding taxes. Federal income tax returns had once been the concern only of the rich. Between 1939 and 1943 the number of federal taxpayers jumped tenfold, and dollar payments rose sixteenfold. Virtually every family now paid income taxes. Popular support for future government spending sprees was undercut, as the beneficiaries of federal largesse learned they would have to pay for it. The conservative Republicans who had long bemoaned rising tax burdens now saw their audiences grow in size. All the big New Deal relief and spending programs were abolished or sharply curtailed, except the Reconstruction Finance Corporation, which financed the conversion of industry to war production.

Illinois sent its share of money to war and devoted its economy to the task at hand. Food production expanded, and transportation worked to capacity. The state's industrial contribution was enormous, though it lacked the glamour of West Coast airplane factories and shipyards. Employment in manufacturing soared throughout the state. The greatest expansion in employment came in ordinance, since the old Rock Island arsenal and newer plants near Joliet and Carbondale supplied much of the firepower of the Allied bombers, battleships, long guns, and rifles. A new shipyard on the Illinois River built landing craft for Pacific warfare, while giant plants in Chicago assembled aircraft engines, and smaller factories built radio and radar equipment. Youth quit school to work in factories. Single women or mothers whose children were in school supported the men at the front by joining the labor force in record numbers. They worked in offices, stores, and laundries; they assembled electronic parts, drove taxicabs, and even took on heavy factory labor that had traditionally been an exclusively male preserve. Without adequate child care facilities, many women found their dual roles as housekeeper and factory worker tiresome and disruptive of home life. Few opportunities for advancement opened to women but the pay was good, the service helped the war effort, and peacetime would be easier.

The spirit of the war was shared sacrifice. A blue star in the window signified a soldier at war; a gold star honored the war dead. Children pasted savings stamps in little books and collected scrap metal and newspapers. Radio, the press, and the movies in particular primed civilian morale with stories first of heroic battles, then of decisive victories. Few despaired of winning the war; America had an unpleasant job to finish and finish quickly. Emotional, crusading propaganda was unnecessary. Hatred was reserved for Hitler and the "Japs."

In 1917–1918, twenty thousand patriots scoured the hillsides and alleyways for lurking saboteurs, spies, or slackers. In the second war, eleven thousand hastily trained aircraft spotters scanned the prairie skies for the first sign of German bombers which might have eluded Indiana, Michigan, or Wisconsin binoculars. None of the false alarms were authenticated. Just in case, though, more than a million citizens enlisted in civil defense, where they rehearsed blackouts, practiced air raid drills, studied first aid, and organized into auxiliary police, fire, medical, and bomb demolition squads. The auxiliary police in Quincy took jujitsu lessons to deal with possible enemy parachutists or blackout offenders. Civil defense took charge after a tornado hit Lacon in Marshall County and a train wrecked near Poplar Grove. The worst floods in a century on the Illinois River and high water on the Mississippi in 1943 and 1944 tested their training and proved the need for emergency civil organization. After the war, disaster plans, permanent auxiliary forces, and a legacy of co-operation provided communities with a margin of safety in the event of natural disaster.

Chicago mobilized its civil defense more thoroughly than any metropolis in America. Block by block some 900,000 volunteers organized to meet any emergency. Nazi bombers never came, of course, but the block and neighborhood organizations soon discovered more valuable functions. The city's ethnics enjoyed the sense of co-operation and full participation in the war effort as air raid wardens made the rounds, children asked for scrap, and neighbors proudly posted stars in their windows. Block meetings dealt with victory gardens, rummage sales, the need for playground equipment, formation of carpools, and breakfasts for departing draftees. More serious issues—rats in decrepit tenements, polluted water, hoarding, ugly rumors, rationing rules, noise abatement, postwar peace aims—all were aired in meetings that forged a new sense of neighborhood identity and civil involvement. Chicago was no longer a great agglomeration of isolated individuals—the proud flags on homemade flagstaffs flew above genuinely close-knit communities that were destined to survive and flourish for decades. The war for survival had become a war of democracy at home.

6

The Suburban Era: Climax and Collapse of Modernity

*T*HE two decades following the Second World War saw another triumph of modern values in Illinois. After the disruptions, frustrations, and heartaches of fifteen years of depression and war, young men and women hurried to make up for lost opportunities. Against a backdrop of steady economic growth in an economy well balanced among agriculture, manufacturing, trade, and services, the steady rise in incomes and wealth again infused the people with self-confidence and optimism that progress would never stop. When unpopular war abroad, soaring crime and violence on the streets, recession, inflation, and discovery of corruption at the highest level engulfed America in the late 1960s and the 1970s, the good cheer evaporated, modern values came into question, and Illinois shared with the nation a sense of confusion and alienation.

These evils were unimagined when the world war ended. Dreams of the good life—so long postponed—were realized with a rush as Illinois entered an era of suburbanization. Financed by higher incomes and a stock of savings built up during the war, both the white- and blue-collar workers were free to enjoy security and self-fulfillment. Automobile ownership in the state doubled between 1945 and the early 1950s, giving nearly all families easy, cheap mobility. The opening of the first subway system in Chicago in 1943 likewise enlarged the range of opportunity of those too poor to own a car, or too nervous to navigate the eight-lane, high-speed expressways that were built in the 1950s and 1960s. Automobiles permitted escape from the crowded apartments and row houses of the inner city for much larger homes in the suburban areas within or beyond the city limits. By 1970, 80 percent of the people lived in the Chicago or downstate metropolitan areas, most of them in suburbs rather than central cities. Hanover Park, a tiny village of 450 souls in 1960, became a dense suburb of 12,000 population ten years later. Naperville, a town older than Chicago itself, doubled in size to 24,000 between 1960 and 1970 as the outward thrust of suburbanization carried farther and farther. By 1970, suburbs were employing more people than the central cities of Illinois. Only half the suburbanites in Du Page County, for example, had to travel outside the county to work. Although they afforded an escape from the dirt, crime, noise, high taxes, crowding, and bad schools of the central city, the suburbs, apart from older places like Alton, Oak Park, and Evanston, lacked cultural amenities and a spirit of community. "I don't spend enough time in Hoffman Estates to even know what's going on," admitted one advertising executive. "To me this is a bedroom community. I'm here just to sack out."

With heavy state and federal investment in highways, and the growth of cable TV networks, the last vestiges of rural and smalltown isolation disappeared. Executives in the Quad Cities discovered the fine schools and stately homes of Geneseo made it an ideal place to raise a family. When Jones and Laughlin built an ultramodern, hundred-million-dollar steel plant in the little hamlet of Hennepin in Grundy County, they knew that the universal ownership of automobiles would permit their employees to commute an average of twenty miles each way without complaint. Indeed, with CB radios everywhere, driving became fun. By 1970 even the people who lived in old farmhouses were not necessarily farmers—more than half were employed in factories, stores, and schools. Urban-rural distinctions vanished as the state became more homogeneous. Indeed, the very term "urban" no longer connoted sophistication, wealth, and diversity; instead it was reserved for the chronic problems of poverty, welfare, crime, and disorder in the inner-city black ghettos of Chicago, East Saint Louis, and Cairo.

Small towns across the state grew more alike as branches of McDonald's, Walgreen's, Sears, A & P, and Midas Muffler provided standard goods and uniform service. Owners of distinctive local establishments yielded to the trend by buying a national franchise and following prescribed styles of operation, by selling out to a conglomerate, or by going out of business. The people of Illinois lived almost exactly the same as those of any other state: the same television, clothing, medical care, automobiles, and household appliances were everywhere, with the remaining differences fading more every year. The consumer, employee, and junior executive alike gained from the increased productivity that resulted from standardization. Few sighs of nostalgia mourned the passing of the inefficient uniqueness of towns and neighborhoods until the historic preservation movement of the 1970s reminded people of what they were fast losing.

Released from the deprivation and anxieties of depression and war, families centered their lifestyle around home and children. The birth rate soared as women eagerly left their wartime jobs to enjoy full-time homemaking and child care. The suburbs were particularly attractive for raising children: schools were better, recreation easier, the streets safer and less tense. Furthermore, taxes were lower, machine politics less evident, government was cleaner and closer to the citizen. The parents were delighted that their tax dollars went for new, modern elementary and high schools, stocked with amenities lacking in the inner city and staffed with younger, more innovative teachers. Suburbs like Evanston, Northfield, Skokie, and Hinsdale competed for the status of having the best schools in the Midwest, an investment more than repaid in higher property values. Residents of small towns, however, seemed especially pleased with Illinois's low tax rates; they preferred larger automobiles at the cost of roads with potholes. Children who sat in cramped, overcrowded classrooms by day would at least enjoy bigger-screen television sets at night.

Education came to be universally recognized as the long-range cure for all social ills, and as a practically guaranteed route to upward mobility for the individual. Modern values reigned unchallenged as state and local governments spent heavily for new buildings, smaller classes, more equipment, finer textbooks, and better-educated and better-paid teachers. The Catholics and German Lutherans made their parochial systems exact imitations of the public systems. By the 1960s, a high school diploma was the routine expectation of every youth in Illinois, and increasing numbers went on to college. Enrollment in higher education grew from 107,000 in 1940 to 164,000 in 1956, then began to soar, reaching 500,000 by the late 1970s. The state upgraded its teachers' colleges into full-scale universities, opened a branch of the University of Illinois in downtown Chicago, and created dozens of community colleges to enable students anywhere in Illinois to live at home and commute to class. While enrollment grew, so did the quality of learning. The students every year were better prepared, more motivated, smarter. The outstanding research universities—Chicago, Illinois, and Northwestern—firmed their international leadership in science, engineering, and medicine, while mushrooming schools like Illinois Institute of Technology and Southern Illinois University won national attention for their excellence in specialized fields.

Whatever the enhancement of lifestyle made possible by continued education, the economic value of additional schooling began to decline as more and more well-educated young alumni began competing for the same jobs. Illinois men who attended college for a year or two in the 1930s and 1940s earned 30 percent more in 1969 than their peers who were graduated from high school but went no further. But the differential was only 6 percent for men who went to college in the 1960s; that is, they earned only $500 a year more than their high school classmates. Similarly, men who won a college degree in the 1930s and 1940s in 1969 earned nearly double the salary of men who only had a high school diploma, but the advantage dropped to only 24 percent for college alumni of the 1960s. College education had become so routine in America that it no longer conferred an automatic advantage. Skilled blue-collar workers and white-collar workers found their incomes increasingly overlapping;

they were neighbors in the same suburbs, drove the same model cars, wore identical clothes, vacationed at the same resorts. The technological sophistication of many blue-collar jobs made these workers practically as modern as white-collar employees doing routine clerical work. Class differences thus were narrowing rapidly in the modern state.

The most drastic step in ridding rural Illinois of traditionalist localism was school consolidation. With 12,000 separate local taxing units in 1942, Illinois had more school districts than any other state. Ten thousand one-room elementary schools remained in the state, with an average enrollment of only a dozen children. Rural depopulation and inefficiency doomed the old system. The 142 rural schools in Pike County had from forty to seventy-five pupils each in 1890, but the 81 remaining in 1947 enrolled from two to twenty-five. Equipment was decrepit; the teachers were badly paid and often had no more than a mediocre high school education. To be sure, the farmers enjoyed the ability to control an important agency of government themselves—in Wayne County, there were 600 elected, but unpaid, district school board members supervising only 217 teachers. Most of the teachers were unmarried young women who lived at home, probably turning their paychecks over to their fathers.

Consolidation would upgrade the quality of education the children received at the cost of higher taxes. Buses, modern buildings, new textbooks, and well-paid, college-educated teachers cost money. Consolidation with villages and towns would subject farmers to much higher school taxes because of the inequitable system of property assessment. Efficiency would be improved by equalizing spending—per pupil costs in Macon County ranged from $85 in one district to $631 in another in 1948—but state financial aid would be required before the farmers accepted the change. The more traditional rural folk worried about the loss of their way of life if control over their children passed into the hands of cosmopolitan educators—strangers who heeded the advice of professors in Chicago or Champaign rather than the wisdom of the crossroads service station. Finally the farm organizations, recognizing the need for modern education for children who would have to compete in a technological society, agreed to a gradual program of consolidation. The number of districts fell from 12,000 to 6,000 in 1948, and finally to only 600 elementary districts in 1978. The state sweetened the development by paying a much larger share of the school budget, and by financing 10,000 buses to transport 800,000 pupils a year. The demise of the last neighborhood institution in rural Illinois was the occasion for nostalgia and concern about the hazards of busing and the loss of neighborhood identity. "I have just begun to realize what our country school means to us," a Christian County woman wrote in 1948. "September is gone and no wiener roast or get-together of any kind. The school was the only place where we farmers could meet once a month and really enjoy ourselves."

Suburbanization in Illinois eradicated most of the differences among ethnic and religious groups, apart from blacks and Spanish. Relatively few immigrants arrived from Europe after 1914, and the older generation was dying out. The children, grandchildren, and great-grandchildren lost most traces of their ethnic heritage, save for occasional festivals. "Let's face it," said a young lawyer in Chicago, "we've had it better than our parents. On St. Patrick's Day we try to identify as Irish, but it's only pretending." True, the older folk still clustered in Polish, Czech, or Italian neighborhoods, but they had abandoned the old language and folkways, and were insistent that their children receive a high school or college education that would prepare them for a fully modern lifestyle, complete with either a white-collar position or a well-paying, skilled blue-collar job. By the 1950s the differences in income among younger, American-born sons and daughters of immigrants had largely evaporated. The Jews—the best-educated, most middle-class group—had the highest incomes, but Irish Catholics were close behind. Yankees still dominated the big banks, prestigious law offices, and posh corporate headquarters in the state, but, taking all Yankees together, they had been surpassed in income and education by several ethnic groups by the 1960s. Blacks, Chicanos, and Puerto Ricans in Illinois, as recent arrivals with few modern skills, fell much below par in income and education. Only one characteristic differentiated Catholics and white Protestants in Illinois: politics. True to the heritage of their parents and grandparents, Catholics preferred the Democratic party by two-to-one, while white Protestants favored the GOP. Jews and blacks continued their overwhelming preference for the liberal Democrats. The candidacy of John F. Kennedy in 1960 reinforced the religious polarization of politics. Kennedy captured 76 percent of the Illinois Catholic vote, 75 percent of the black, and 83 percent of the Jewish. But he won only 34 percent of the Methodist, 23 percent of the Lutheran, and 19 percent of the Presbyterian and Episcopalian vote. Despite the anti-Catholicism latent in the 1960 campaign, religious prejudice vanished rapidly after Kennedy entered the White House and demonstrated that old fears of papist traditionalism were groundless.

With the steady movement toward modern attitudes and values among Catholics, the Democratic party was forced to abandon its most traditionalistic characteristics (except in machine-dominated black neighborhoods). It became more middle class in orientation until its programs at the state and local level were virtually indistinguishable from those of the Republicans. Efficiency, anticorruption, and business-style government were slogans as easily tripped off in Democratic as Republican rallies. The change in the Democratic party became noticeable immediately after the war. The Republican landslide of 1946, which even swept Chicago, convinced Democrats that they had to adopt a reform image and, in fact, actually support reform. Long-term Chicago Mayor Edward Kelly, the personification of traditional machine politics, was dumped in 1947 in favor of a blue-ribbon businessman. In 1948 two distinguished reformers, Paul Douglas and Adlai Stevenson, were elected to the Senate and the governorship, respectively. Stevenson's success triggered the formation of a liberal reform movement within the Democratic party, eventually culminating in the election of Governor Daniel Walker as the crusader battling the Cook County Democratic organization.

Stevenson was an ineffective governor. Temperamentally he could not co-operate with local or legislative leaders; his real interest was in international affairs. His major achievement was use of state law enforcement officials to destroy syndicated gambling–prostitution–loan shark rings in Rock Island, Peoria, Joliet, Decatur, Springfield, and even in the notorious East Saint Louis region. Except in the last area, organized vice remained suppressed, and local politics took a quantum leap away from the corrupt linkages between the underworld and politicians. Traditionalist politicians were replaced with efficient administrative experts.

In the middle and late 1960s a series of modernist reforms produced a striking improvement in the quality of state government. Reapportionment, the destruction of the "west side block" of corrupt Chicago Republican legislators, improved staffing, and the weakening of old lobbies improved the legislature to such an extent that a national review panel judged it third in the country in effectiveness. During Republican Richard Ogilvie's term as governor (1969–1972), management "whiz kids" revitalized the executive bureaucracy, brought the budget under control, and co-ordinated the fast-growing higher education complex. A new income tax doubled the state's revenues between 1968 and 1971, providing more state money for local schools and law enforcement. Federal revenue sharing eased the fiscal problems of local government and permitted the introduction of long-range planning, modern budgeting and capital outlay management, more sophisticated administrators, and more efficient, higher-quality service to the public. Other federal programs, notably Medicaid for the elderly, festered as a national scandal.

In Cook County, leaders of the dominant Democratic organization realized that modernization of local government was necessary to maintain the support of an increasingly middle-class constituency. The suburban Cook County schools achieved the reputation as the best in the United States. The quality of Chicago's public schools invariably deteriorated as the middle classes moved to the suburbs, their children replaced with minority children whose family, economic, and cultural environment was scarcely conducive to learning. Nevertheless, at Mayor Daley's insistence the city poured resources into the schools until its teachers were the best paid in the country. Compared with other big cities, the teachers were more likely to meet with parents; despite deteriorating buildings the teachers rated Chicago fifth in overall quality among fifteen comparable big-cities school systems in 1968. Citizens ranked the city's schools in the middle, a rather optimistic judgment.

Chicago police were notoriously corrupt in the 1950s, routinely accepting ten-dollar bribes from traffic offenders or vastly larger kickbacks from nightclubs, brothels, and gambling shops. In 1960 public scandals forced Daley to take drastic action. An outside reformer cracked down on the petty corruption; shook up the old-boy network of promotions; modernized equipment, training, and procedures; raised salaries and morale; and sharply improved services. By 1968 Chicago ranked second among fifteen large cities in satisfactory police service, according to both blacks and whites, and won the praise of law enforcement professionals across the country.

Chicago was proud of its ability to handle the challenges of recession, poverty, massive black and Spanish immigration, middle-class suburban exodus, labor strife, physical blight, air pollution, racial conflict, political corruption, and, indeed, every other ill then facing big cities. Routine services—police, fire, sanitation, mass transport, education—were better than average, and the level of debt and taxation stayed within bounds. Industry did not flee the area; the great skyscrapers of the Loop testified to Chicago's continued business vitality, and the multiplication of luxury apartments and condominiums along the lakefront proved its attractiveness for young white-collar workers and professionals. Anyone who compared the city with New York, Philadelphia, Detroit, Saint Louis, or Boston could only marvel at Chicago's success.

Observers agreed that the key was the political harmony forged by Richard Daley's Cook County Democratic organization. As powerful as any machine the country has known, it forced city, county, state, and even federal government officials to co-ordinate their planning and spending. More important, Daley's close-knit network of Irish politicians served as the communication bridge among all sorts of diverse groups. Chicago's rich and poor, blacks, Poles, Italians, Germans, Jews, Chicanos, Puerto Ricans, Czechs, Scandinavians, Slovaks, and Yankees, educators, world bankers, industrialists, labor unions, and real estate developers could reach each other only by going through Irish intermediaries. Each group put its trust in Daley, and in turn received at least part of what it wanted. Above all, conflicts that elsewhere produced burning hatreds, soaring taxes, drawn-out strikes, or simple disgust could be resolved through the mayor's good offices. No wonder Daley won landslide re-election time after time. The question in 1978 was whether his loss would fragment the city politically and economically, producing a void in leadership that would leave Chicago open to chaos.

The wartime spirit of national unity and common sacrifice carried over into the cold war years. The heavy wartime tax burden lightened only partly because the threat of war with Russia produced virtual unanimity that high defense spending was necessary. The concept of national defense proved elastic enough to justify massive federal spending, beginning in the late 1950s, on the interstate highway system. The financial damage it inflicted on the state's railroads was more than offset by the impetus to the trucking industry and the growth of suburbs. Psychologically, the cold war threat unified all segments of the population. Labor unions vied with chambers of commerce in denunciations of communism. Although considerable support for Wisconsin Sen. Joe McCarthy existed in Illinois, it rarely took the form of witch-hunting or book burning. Illinois expressed its anticommunism by identifying the Red menace with violation of modern values such as freedom of speech and religion. Capitalism, seen as a benign co-operation among businessmen, labor, and consumers, became identified with Americanism. The greatest benefit of capitalism, hence of Americanism, was considered to be freedom to enjoy the fruits of modernity. Wealth, security, and religious tolerance were the promised rewards of the American way of life. Class conflict diminished sharply in Illinois after a wave of strikes in 1946 confirmed unions' rights to represent industrial and crafts workers in collective bargaining. Seniority, insurance and pension plans, and the state's high wages and low unemployment guaranteed security for blue-collar workers that previously only the middle classes had enjoyed. Automobiles, refrigerators, radio consoles and television sets were universal in every neighborhood, even the poorest slums. Comfort, security, and the promise of continued progress—all blessed by a benign, noncontroversial, religious faith—made the suburban era a time of placid complacency. No one seemed to mind the increasingly complex bureaucratic work environments, nor did opposition emerge to the self-discipline modern society demanded. Memories of the harsh depression years were so firmly implanted that a strict adherence to modernity seemed the only way to live. The children of the baby boom of the 1940s and 1950s, however, were reared in affluence and remembered neither the shared hardships of the depression nor the rousing nationalism of the war years. When they came of age in the 1960s and 1970s, they were hypersensitive to the contradictions of modernity—shortcomings their parents could not see. The offspring of modernity and affluence were ready to introduce new values to America.

By the late 1960s Illinois began experiencing a disquieting shift in values. Old norms of repressed sexual behavior suddenly gave way; respect for authority declined sharply both in private and public sectors; confidence in the future gave way to anxiety. A new set of values, which we must call "postmodern," began emerging, values that grew out of both the traditional and modern norms we have been tracing, but were distinct from them. Everyone was affected to some extent, though the most dramatic changes appeared among blacks, youth, Catholics, and career women.

Illinois blacks had never accepted the second-class citizenship forced upon them by segregation. On the one hand the white supremacy of southern and ethnic traditionalists squeezed the blacks into ghettoes where poverty, crime, and ignorance flourished. On the other hand, the middle-class whites were repelled by the disorder of the ghettoes. Apart from a few reformers who sought to modernize blacks through education and social work, the middle classes were content to ignore the problem. It grew worse. Between 1940 and 1970 the black population of Illinois tripled from 400,000 to 1,400,000. The majority were wedged into dilapidated housing on the south or west sides of Chicago, but ghettoes of ten to fifteen thousand blacks had formed in Champaign-Urbana, the Quad Cities, Decatur, Rockford, Joliet, and Evanston, with 76,000 more in the East Saint Louis ghetto.

The small but rapidly growing middle-class black population keenly resented its inferior status, particularly its lack of access to adequate housing. As the ghettoes became overcrowded the wealthier blacks moved into previously all-white neighborhoods. The result was usually white panic and either whole-sale departure or defensive violence. The whites in the path of black expansion were usually working-class ethnics with strong neighborhood ties, unhappy memories of black strikebreakers, fear of the extremely high ghetto crime rates, and an implicit feeling that blacks were hopelessly traditional in morals, behavior, and lifestyle.[1] The middle-class blacks who were themselves trying to escape the disorders of the ghetto bitterly resented the unfair stereotypes the whites applied to them. They especially resented white unwillingness to integrate their schools, whose facilities and learning environments were vastly superior to those of ghetto schools.

Racial problems became the focus of national attention in the early 1960s. The system of legal discrimination against blacks in the South clearly violated the universalistic premise of the modernist creed, as embedded in the Fourteenth Amendment. The plight of middle-class blacks who were denied equal opportunity in jobs, housing, and politics roused the consciences of ministers, intellectuals, labor union leaders, and politicians. With Sen. Everett Dirksen playing a key role, Congress enacted a series of civil rights laws that were widely applauded in Illinois. Whites thought they would apply only to the South. Most Illinois blacks apparently were loyal allies of the Democratic organization, which tried to accommodate them with welfare money, public housing, and a modest share of political power. When civil rights groups began protesting segregated housing and schools in Chicago, city hall mobilized its black ministers and precinct workers to affirm their loyalty to the establishment. Dr. Martin Luther King, Jr., came to Chicago to rally the dissidents but made little headway. His threats to lead marchers into all-white ethnic neighborhoods, particularly Cicero, cost

---

1. In Chicago in 1965, crimes against persons were four times higher in low-income black neighborhoods than in low-income white neighborhoods; crimes against property were 30 percent higher, yet the black neighborhoods had double the number of patrolmen. Except for armed robbery, which is usually a black-on-white crime, the victims and criminals were normally of the same race. Since white victims more often had insurance, they reported crimes more regularly. Thus the true differential between white and black crime rates was even higher than official statistics indicated.

him the support of most whites, and he left Chicago in frustration.

Civil rights laws were designed to help middle-class blacks. The larger mass of poverty-stricken, lower-class blacks were ignored until they began to riot in 1964. A series of "long hot summers" showed white America that acceptance of modernist blacks would not meet the grievances of the ghetto. As Watts, Newark, Detroit, and Cleveland burned, the federal government reacted by funnelling hundreds of millions of dollars into a "war on poverty." Much of the money went to street gangs (in effect, buying them off), to legal aid programs, and to ill-advised "model city" projects that proved a windfall for real estate speculators. Most money went to increased welfare. Aid to families with dependent children (mostly black) doubled between 1959 and 1965, doubled again by 1968, and soared to $600 million in Illinois in 1973. By 1978 the state spent $2 billion a year on welfare. The old ideal of welfare, to uplift deserving poor to a modern value system and lifestyle, gave way to a postmodern ideal: the poor should be subsidized regardless of the causes or the consequences. This change in policy also implied vast sums for the aged, who finally received enough aid to maintain a semblance of dignity and comfort.

Previously, middle-class Negroes had demanded their civil rights and an opportunity to integrate themselves into modern society. Now younger, angrier ghetto youth called for black power, an end to police harassment, rights for prisoners, and increased welfare payments. The new demands were postmodern in tone and caught white Illinois by surprise. It had just agreed to extend the privileges of modernity to qualified Negroes, only to discover the ghetto wanted something else. Modern political procedures—voting, court tests, intellectual and sentimental appeals to the principles of equal rights and fair play—gave way to postmodern tactics of direct confrontation, threats of violence, and riots in the street. "Burn, baby, burn!" was replacing the text of the Fourteenth Amendment as the lever for change. Violence flared briefly on Chicago's West Side in 1966, and in Cairo, East Saint Louis, Peoria, Rockford, and Elgin in 1967. Racial tension continued to mount in Chicago.

The explosion came in April 1968, in the wake of Dr. King's assassination. Three days of rioting, looting, and arson erupted on Chicago's West Side. Seven thousand National Guard troops, reinforced by 5,000 federal soldiers, finally restored calm after 3,000 arrests, 500 injuries, and 9 deaths. Violence on a much smaller scale occurred simultaneously in Evanston, Maywood, East Saint Louis, Alton, Joliet, Aurora, Carbondale, and Chicago Heights, not to mention a hundred other cities across the United States.

The ghetto riots were symbolic affairs, more a psychological declaration of independence on the part of lower-class blacks than a systematic effort to kill or injure. Except in Cairo, where intense white resistance led to years of intermittent violence and escalating hatreds, the ghetto riots were short, intensive outbursts, and whites left countermeasures to the police and the National Guard. The riots proved their point quickly and required no repetition. In the aftermath blacks discovered a new sense of unity—expressed in the slogan "Black Power," and made concrete by efforts to enlarge the sphere of black economic and political influence.

East Saint Louis, with a collapsing economy, was a tinderbox. Lamented the Episcopal rector, "It's a doomed city because of crooked politicians, a mobster element, apathy of the man in the street, a very high unemployment rate—especially among Negroes, who are now in a majority—and because potentially responsible white leadership has moved out to the suburbs." A poverty leader noted that "every black man in town supports the disturbances. Who's to say the violent way is wrong? Let's see what it accomplishes." In 1971 a reform slate of black leaders took control of city hall from the old white-controlled machine and began working with white elites to save the city from total collapse and chaos.

Although independent black power movements brought about election of mayors in Atlanta, Cleveland, Detroit, Gary, Los Angeles, and Newark, the pattern in Chicago was continued collaboration with the Cook County Democratic organization. The reward was a share of power in the city council and the state legislature, and immense amounts of patronage. In Ralph Metcalfe's South Side district, ten thousand blacks held well-paid, nonstrenuous city or county jobs in the late 1970s. "Patronage in Chicago isn't some trifling thing—it's an industry," explained a black editor. "And political jobs mean more to blacks than whites because blacks don't have all that much opportunity elsewhere." Jesse Jackson, the militant spokesman of the upwardly mobile, more modern blacks, attacked Daley sharply, but had far more success in convincing grocery chains, breweries, and other industries with large black clienteles to hire more blacks, to upgrade their jobs, and to do more business with black-owned establishments. Only Congressman Metcalfe had the prestige to lead an independent effort in Chicago, but he was a trusted lieutenant in the machine until he finally broke with Daley in 1973 on the issue of police brutality. "It's never too late for a Negro to become black," Metcalfe noted during his desperate 1976 re-election effort. His organization opponent, affirming that he, too, believed in liberation, added, "I've never seen a man who was liberated who didn't have a job, or some money in his pocket, or a decent place to live." Metcalfe's stunning victory proved that the Daley Democrats could no longer count on huge automatic majorities from the ghetto.

Across the state initial white reaction to the riots was intensely hostile, for the rioters violated the norms of modern conduct. "When I see on TV those demonstrators it makes me think of them as savages," snapped a Joliet housewife. "They're dirty. They get housing projects and in two years they look like dumps." Mayor Daley ordered police to shoot arsonists and looters—they did not do so, but panicky whites rushed to buy handguns to protect their homes. On Chicago's southwest side Francis Lawlor, a Catholic priest, began to organize a network of 150 block clubs to halt the ghetto's expansion at Ashland Avenue. "You are the product of all these centuries of civilized living," he told his Polish, Irish, and Italian supporters, "and the civilized cannot let themselves be overrun by the uncivilized." White support for civil rights legislation collapsed and a backlash vote emerged. George Wallace captured 30 percent of the white Cairo vote in 1968, while the white Chicago wards that were targets of Dr. King's marches switched from 66 percent Democratic in 1960 to 42 percent in 1968. Two-thirds of the Italians and Poles felt personally uneasy about racial violence, compared to only a third of the white Protestants, who lived in quiet towns and suburbs. Incumbent Sen. Paul Douglas bore the brunt of the backlash for his outspoken support of civil rights laws, and he was defeated by Republican Charles Percy in 1966.[2]

After the ghetto riots ended in 1968 Illinois white leaders re-evaluated their stances. Universities recruited poorly prepared black students and, along with the high schools, began offering courses designed to highlight black pride. Businesses promoted and retrained their black employees and worked to reduce white hostility. Father Lawlor, now a Chicago alderman, found ways to co-operate with black leaders to ease the anguish of change in his ward. By the early 1970s young, well-educated black families were earning more money than their white counterparts, and were increasingly accepted in middle-class jobs and neighborhoods. Ghetto conditions for the poor blacks remained grim; although vastly increased welfare payments eased their plight, violent crime also soared. "I'd like to move out of this neighborhood," mused one Chicago janitor. "Maybe I'll go back South, where you can walk the streets in the dark without carrying a pistol in your pocket all the time." And, "I hope my boys can make it through their teens without killing somebody or getting themselves killed," prayed one mother. A black steel mill worker felt "the worst thing is children taking dope, escaping from the nothingness that is all they have to look forward to."

The faith that modernists had always placed in universal education as the way to eradicate the crime, drug abuse, and proclivity toward violence, gambling, and improvidence among traditional youth was severely shaken in the wake of the riots. True, the aspiring middle-class blacks could use this route to escape, but it did not seem to be working for the majority. The schools themselves were filled with drugs, gangs, contempt for learning, and violence. Teachers were often no more than custodians, waiting until they had enough seniority to transfer to a middle-class neighborhood. Nineteen sixty-nine was a particularly violent year. Violent racial confrontations hit nineteen Chicago

---

2. Percy himself supported civil rights. In defeating a Polish opponent in 1972, he was the only Republican in the country to carry a majority of the black vote.

high schools, with 300 injuries and 340 arrests; in April 7,000
National Guard troops were ordered to the city. Suburban and
downstate high schools also experienced disorder, including
those in Alton, Blue Island, Chicago Heights, Evanston, Har-
vey, Kankakee, Madison, Maywood, Midlothian, Rockford,
Springfield, and Zion. The violence eventually burned out, but
not before stimulating intense white resistance to compulsory
busing proposals for integration in Rockford, Kankakee, and
elsewhere. In Chicago, where barely a fourth of the public
school students were white in 1978, meaningful racial integration was a hopeless proposition, and blacks focused their efforts
on community control of the schools.

Before the 1960s, high schools avoided violence by simply
expelling "troublemakers." The extension of modern rights of
due process to students foreclosed that solution, and the rising
militance of youth made conflict inevitable. At a deeper level
than racial tension, a value shift was occurring among youth.
They no longer automatically accepted authority figures, demanding instead recognition of their rights to control their own
lives and a share in making decisions. The goals that once justified obedience—the need to study in order to acquire modern
skills, the superior knowledge of teachers, a basic belief in the
importance of science and scholarship—were no longer of paramount importance. Imitations of lower-class use of drugs and
alcohol, free sexual experimentation, long hair, rock music, and
modish dress became the style of the postmodern culture. As-
trology replaced science; intense experiences—whether sexual,
mystical, or violent—replaced discipline; the quest for autonomy
displaced acceptance of well-charted careerism. Anxiety about
pollution, disgust with racism, militarism, the draft, and the
Vietnam War, profound cynicism about politics after the assassinations of the Kennedys and Dr. King—all combined to produce a revulsion against the modern, bureaucratic, technological
social order.

Postmodern youth, animated by opposition to the undeclared,
indecisive war in Vietnam, and alienated from anything that
smacked of the modern establishment, brought the politics of
confrontation to the Democratic National Convention in Chicago in the summer of 1968. City police broke up the demon-

strations with a show of force that Dan Walker, in an official report, termed a "police riot." Most adults, particularly the skilled blue-collar workers, or "hard hats," who had only recently become modernized, applauded the police. A long trial of the demonstration leaders turned the federal courtroom in Chicago into a comic-absurd confrontation between the postmodern challenge of "The Chicago Seven" and the unyielding modern values of the prosecutor and Judge Julius Hoffman. All the defendants were eventually freed, indicating that the mood of the state was shifting rapidly. In 1972 the postmoderns had their revenge on Daley by ousting him and his entire delegation from the Democratic National Convention. George McGovern carried the postmodern banner into presidential politics, only to be totally demolished by Richard Nixon's call for a return to the modern ethic.

To be sure, not all youth immediately adopted postmodern values. The trend began among elite college students from wealthy, liberal backgrounds, gained strength from black ghetto lifestyles, and slowly spread to youth who never were expected to go to college. In the late 1970s a partial reaction was noticeable, as elite students at Northwestern, Knox, Urbana, Lake Forest, Chicago, and elsewhere abandoned the more fantastic aspects of the postmodern style (like communes) and reverted to intensive preparation for medical or law school. Even so, they scorned the quiet, lucrative careers of their elders and talked of devoting themselves to public interest law, Ralph Nader–style, or to providing medical care for the hungry poor instead of the obese rich. Nevertheless a drastic change in beliefs, values, and behavior did occur among a large portion of youth. Adults who were at first alarmed and disgusted learned to tolerate long hair, nudity, rock concerts, sexual freedom, even marijuana smoking, though they rarely experimented themselves. In every sector of society, sharp age differentials emerged in the 1960s, pitting the modernist middle-aged against the postmodern youth. The former were alarmed at the anarchy of youth, their disregard of the "lessons" of the past (i.e., those of the 1930s and 1940s), and their unwillingness to work peacefully for change in institutions that were thoroughly controlled by the middle-aged. A good example of the impact of postmodern, antiauthoritarian search for personal autonomy came in the realm of religion.

Roman Catholics, constituting a third of the state's population, had long set themselves apart. Most were ethnics—German, Irish, Polish, Lithuanian, Czech, Slovak, Puerto Rican, or Chicano—accustomed to crowded city living and low-paying manual jobs and familiar with the painful adjustments immigrants had to make in America. They attended Mass faithfully on Sunday, participating in an elaborate Latin ritual that was controlled entirely by a priest set above the laity by his sacred powers. Catholic children attended parochial schools where devout nuns inculcated faith in sacraments, miracles, and the infallible supremacy of the pope. Catholics and Protestants mingled little in Illinois—even those Catholics who had attended public schools chose Catholics for friends and marriage partners. For the entire history of the state the Catholics voted for the Democrats as the party of traditionalism and the opponent of aggressive Protestant reformism.

Change came dramatically in the 1960s. Ethnicity, as we have seen, faded in importance. The election of John Kennedy as president symbolized the final, long-delayed acceptance of Catholics in the community. Anti-Catholicism decayed and Catholics took fresh pride in their adoption of modern lifestyles and values. Pope John XXIII and the Second Vatican Council then reorganized the rituals of the church, abandoning traditional practices such as Latin Masses and meatless Fridays. The authoritarianism of the church loosened somewhat, as laymen, nuns, and junior priests gained a small voice in an organization once ruled totally by strong-minded bishops and pastors. With typical American efficiency, the Chicago archdiocese trained 10,000 lay Bible commentators and readers in six weeks, and on the appointed day every altar in the state was turned around to face the people. The revolution from traditionalism to modernity upset some of the older, less-educated Catholics, especially Italians and Spanish. Unexpectedly, John's successor, Pope Paul VI, halted the drift toward liberalizing the traditional bans on divorce, priestly marriage, and, especially, birth control.

Younger Catholics—laity, priests, and nuns alike—reacted sharply. Between the mid-1960s and the early 1970s weekly Mass attendance plunged from 70 to 50 percent, and monthly confessions, daily prayer, and other liturgical practices fell off sharply. The chief reason was the refusal of the hierarchy to approve divorce and birth control, despite the wishes of the laity. Finding it harder to mediate between their parishoners and bishops, younger priests left the church, and few youth entered seminaries. The sisterhood was devastated. In 1962, ten Illinois women became nuns for every one that died or quit. By 1967 the ratio was equal, and by 1969 five left the convent for each new entry. The impact was severe on the Catholic parochial system, which long had depended on nuns working for very low salaries. Half the religious teachers in Illinois disappeared between 1965 and 1978, forcing a one-third cutback in enrollments, the hiring of expensive lay teachers, and sharp tuition increases. Efforts to provide state support for parochial schools failed in the face of stiff opposition from Baptists, Presbyterians, Jews, and the United States Supreme Court.

The upheavals in the church destroyed much of the distinctiveness of Catholicism. Apart from the distinctively ethnic newcomers from Mexico and Puerto Rico, Catholics became almost indistinguishable from their white Protestant neighbors in values, attitudes, and lifestyle. They were still more likely to vote Democratic, and were a shade more favorable toward blacks, unions, gambling, liquor and drugs, and federal spending, and had been somewhat more dovish on Vietnam. (Catholics were much less liberal than blacks or Jews, however.) Young Catholics differed from young Protestants only in very slight ways (e.g., they preferred larger families, though still much smaller than their parents). As the older generation retires, it appears the Illinois Catholic church will become just another denomination more concerned with internal power struggles and value conflicts than with presenting a united front to a hostile world.

The Protestant denominations, meanwhile, experienced their own crises. The heavy involvement of younger clergy and national leaders in the civil rights movement upset both older clergy and a majority of the membership. The more modern denominations—Methodists, Presbyterians, Episcopalians, Disciples of Christ—stopped growing, and provided less and less guidance for their members. By the late 1960s, laymen and clergy alike agreed that organized religion's influence in American life had declined noticeably. What expansion did occur was enjoyed by born-again evangelicals and fundamentalist bodies such as the Southern Baptists, Pentecostals, Jehovah's Witnesses, and Nazarenes. Their highly traditional message of personal salvation above all else caught a receptive audience in a population tired of relentless modernization. Jimmy Carter was their hero, and his reintroduction of traditional religion into politics in 1976 disquieted mainline, modern denominations. Resurgent traditionalists in the larger, basically German, Missouri Synod Lutheran Church took the counteroffensive against "modern" errors (like figurative interpretation of the Old Testament), leading to bitter schism in the mid 1970s. "The church needs a heresy trial!" cried one minister. "A Missouri Synod Lutheran who refuses to accept Holy Scriptures as absolute, immutable truth in every respect is a contradiction in terms." By every standard, the historic, aggressive force of the Protestant modernizers had petered out in Illinois, with scant hope for revival soon.

The equalitarian thrust in the postmodern ethic inevitably raised questions about the status of women in society. Since 1957 the birth rate had fallen steadily, until by the mid-1970s fewer children were being born than were required to replace their parents. Smaller families and a growing economy permitted more mothers to take full- or part-time paid jobs. By 1978, 47 percent of all married women held paid jobs, compared to 24 percent in 1950. Although a Louis Harris poll in 1970 showed that most of the employed women in Illinois were working primarily to bring in extra money (51 percent) or "to keep busy" (11 percent), a significant minority were supporting themselves (23 percent) or their fatherless families (15 percent). Among the latter groups, and especially among college-educated or divorced women, urgent demands arose for equality in employment, training, and pay scales. Old barriers fell as women entered new careers in police work, construction, truck driving, management—even coal mining and the military.

Although the 1970 state constitution forbade discrimination based on sex, and federal laws put teeth in the drive toward equal opportunity, the more militant feminists demanded a federal "Equal Rights Amendment" to guarantee the permanence of their gains. Swift nationwide passage seemed assured until the Illinois legislature unexpectedly rejected the measure. Phyllis Schlafly, an Alton housewife and prominent Republican, had successfully mobilized thousands of housewives wearing old-style long dresses and handing out homemade apple pies in a late-starting countercrusade. Taking advantage of the widespread feeling that postmodern values were eroding family life, Schlafly denounced ERA as "an antifamily movement that is trying to make perversion acceptable as an alternate life-style." "In my scale of values," she explained, "home, family and husband come first."

Advocates and opponents of ERA agreed that the issue was largely symbolic. Both sides favored legislation guaranteeing equal rights to women in specific areas such as work rules and education. The real question was whether the nineteenth-century division of sex roles into separate male and female spheres would give way to a postmodern elimination of the distinction. As noted in chapter two, the two-sphere concept was the modernist solution to the challenge of bringing equality into what had been a totally male-dominated, traditional world. In the 1970s, growing proportions of younger, better-educated women rejected the notion that they should find fulfillment and happiness as housewives and mothers. They had the talent to be doctors, lawyers, bankers, professors, and executives, and were furious at the fact that men held virtually all the top decision-making jobs in every sector of government and economy. While they spoke vaguely of giving women a choice between full equality or protected dominance in the home, the feminists overlooked the fact that housewives, especially older ones, enjoyed their security and luxuries, as well as superior legal advantages in matters of alimony and child custody in case of divorce. "If you want to make your own deal with your boyfriend, fine," Schlafly advised young women, "but why take away the right to be supported of a wife who went into marriage 30 or 40 years ago?"

In 1978 the future of ERA was in doubt, but the pendulum clearly had swung to the opponents. Exponents of postmodern values, with their superior access to the news media, had won the first round. When Schlafly and her housewives finally mobilized their superior numbers, the men who run legislatures—and who vowed to follow women's wishes on this one—discovered the conflict between modern and postmodern values was more complex than it first appeared. If the trend toward careerism and away from home and child-centered family life persists, the feminists seem certain to secure their opportunities, with or without a constitutional amendment.

The faith of the people in "modern" solutions to social problems eroded deeply in the late 1960s and early 1970s. Science, education, engineering, and computerized management made some of their most spectacular advances, symbolized by the landing of a man on the moon, at the same time confidence in these techniques was collapsing. In Illinois as everywhere in the United States, people complained that leaders of technology, education, law, government, labor, religion, and business were out of touch with the society's needs. Two-thirds agreed that these leaders "don't understand people want better quality of almost everything they have, rather than more quantity." Most depressing was the majority opinion that "the quality of leadership, inside and outside of government in this country" had become worse between 1965 and 1975.

In the early 1970s confidence in government plunged to new lows. The Watergate scandal, drummed home daily through intensive media coverage, destroyed long-standing faith in the honesty of the White House. Exposés of the failures of the military (in Vietnam), the CIA, and the FBI further eroded trust in once-hallowed institutions. The federal courts came in for intensive criticism for their decisions in school busing, abortion, and the rights of crime suspects. The reputation of Congress, which seemed impotent in solving the crises of inflation, recession, and energy shortages, fell below even the presidency. State and local government was hardly immune. A Republican ex-governor went to trial; two judges of the state supreme court resigned in disgrace; when Secretary of State Paul Powell died, he left shoeboxes filled with a million dollars of suspicious origins; ex-Governor Otto Kerner went to jail for accepting race track bribes. The once-invincible Cook County Democratic organization reeled under the intensive investigations of federal District

Attorney James Thompson, with several key Democratic party leaders going to prison. Even Richard Daley was touched with hints of scandal when special favors to his sons were uncovered.

The popular response to scandal was not a new citizens' crusade for clean government. Too often that had been tried. Instead cynicism mounted, and apathy resulted. The only hope, in the minds of many citizens who still bothered to vote, was to shrink government. Dan Walker won the governorship in 1972 by denouncing both the Daley machine and the state income tax, levied first in 1969. Taxpayers felt that soaring welfare costs and rising pay scales were absorbing all the new funds, leaving no new services to justify their sacrifices. Walker was a poor administrator and feuded continually with both Democrats and Republicans. Yet he gained grass roots support as he articulated the popular middle-America mood that "government is taking care of *them,* but not me." No matter that administrative and constitutional reforms had greatly enhanced the competence and efficiency of the legislature and the bureaucracy. The problem was that it had become unresponsive. Suburban schoolboards, for example, increasingly lost control of decisions on financing, curriculum, and personnel to state and federal officials, the courts, and powerful teachers' unions. Another loss for popular democracy. The people, alienated by strikes of teachers, police, and other public employees, and by widely publicized scandals, could only see failure. "You can hit on one thing," protested a Winnetka doctor in 1973, "local government will attract people who are not well trained, are political hangers-on, and are more interested in collecting their pay than doing a job." "The healthy skepticism which once invigorated our politics is in danger of becoming a deadly cynicism," sighed Sen. Adlai Stevenson, in explaining why he would not enjoy running for national office in the bicentennial year.

History cannot foretell the future, but it can provide an analytical context for understanding how our present society came to exist, and the process by which one set of dominant values replaces another. Conflict, conversion, and demographic displacement are the mechanisms for such shifts. Illinois has always been large enough to allow diversity. The southern traditionalists of Egypt could have coexisted peacefully with the Yankee modernizers were it not for the natural arena of conflict provided by state and national politics. If democracy means "the people shall rule," then it means that differences in values will have to be resolved by politics—or if that fails, by civil war. Conflict at the polls will be decisive only if the losers accept the verdict. Fortunately, the democratic faith has always been strong enough in Illinois to allow graceful defeat. The losers, instead of plotting assassinations and coups d'etat, or fleeing the state (as the Mormons did in the 1840s), responded with reactionary movements.[3] Thus the racism of antiwar Democrats in the 1860s, the agrarianism of William Jennings Bryan in 1896, and the call for reaffirmation of modern virtues by Ronald Reagan in 1976 were political responses to the success of new models of behavior. Was it coincidence that Bryan and Reagan were both reared in small towns in Illinois, one in Egypt, the other in Yankee Whiteside County, or was this another indication that Illinois was a microcosm of the entire nation?

Conversion is a slower but more certain method of changing social values. The modernists, with their evangelical sense of duty to foment change, tried to convert traditionalists by controlling the public school system and outlawing liquor, drugs, gambling, prostitution, and corruption. Their real success, however, came in the wake of depressions and wars, when traditionalists who sought security and comfort discovered the only sure way to those goals was the acquisition of skills that were in demand in a technological society. When, in the 1970s, the promise of continuous economic growth and added luxury began to seem hollow, the advocates of relaxation of striving and inner discipline began to win their points. With the advent of no-fault insurance and divorce (in practice if not in name), systematic plea bargaining, a new concept of the right to privacy, the selection of juries on the basis of psychological or sociological profiles, and the hiring of policemen on the basis of racial and sexual quotas, it was clear that the old, modern legal

---

3. The term "reactionary" has an ugly ring to the modern ear; here it only means a deliberate effort to restore older values.

norms had given way to a postmodern standard. Legalized gambling, massage parlors, abortion, open homosexuality, and general tolerance for hard-core pornography and soft drugs indicated the end of modern proscriptions, while the conviction of elected government officials for "conflict of interest" marked the beginning of a new ethical standard. State legislation mandating bilingual education, beginning in 1976, in every school enrolling twenty or more students for whom English was not the first language, signalled the replacement of the modern insistence on a homogeneous society by a new form of pluralism. Soaring medical malpractice awards, legalization of quack remedies like laetrile, distrust of giant oil, automobile, and utility corporations, and cutbacks in higher education symbolized the rejection of expertise. A greater concern with pollution than with new steel mills, and with safety rather than cheap nuclear power demonstrated that the goal of economic growth regardless of social cost has lost its appeal. Strikes by teachers, sanitation workers, hospital interns, postal employees, and even policemen prove that government jobs have lost their special prestige and immunity from unionization. Surely the rampant nostalgia during the 1970s for a bygone era, peaking in the bicentennial celebrations of the past, was the signal that millions of people recognized the end of the modern era.

How far society will move toward full acceptance of the postmodern ethic is problematical, but a clue comes from the third and slowest, source of change, demographic displacement. The movement of southern pioneers into Egypt, of Yankees to northern Illinois, of immigrants and blacks to the cities all produced shifts in the locus of political power and in the values and lifestyles of the population. It might seem that no new groups are now moving into Illinois, since the influx of blacks and Latinos has levelled off, but this is an illusion. The generation born after 1940 is the carrier of postmodern values, and its members make up an ever-growing proportion of the decision-makers, more so since the 18-year-olds have had the vote. In 1970 this cohort comprised a quarter of the adult population in Illinois; in 1980 it will comprise half; in 1990, two-thirds. Its values will inevitably come to dominate, whether the dwindling number of older people like it or not. Happily, one core postmodern value is hostility to coercion, reinforced by a celebration of pluralism, with different people allowed to "do their own thing." Moderns and traditionalists, neither very comfortable with diversity in their day, will be able to practice their quaint faith in an atmosphere of bemused tolerance in postmodern Illinois.

Suggestions for Further Reading

Illinois must be visited to be appreciated. Whether exploring by automobile or easy chair, Harry Hansen, *Illinois: A Descriptive and Historical Guide* (New York: Hastings House, 1974) is an invaluable guide to every small town, suburb, or Chicago landmark. The state has taken good care of its artifacts and memorabilia, particularly in the Illinois State Museum in Springfield, the museum of the Chicago Historical Society, and the faithful reconstruction of Lincoln's New Salem, north of Springfield. The text and remarkable illustrations in William Carter, *Middle West Country* (Boston: Houghton Mifflin Co., 1975) an evocative interpretation of the history and culture of the rural heartland. For an up-to-date, accurate, and highly detailed history of the state from the Ice Age to the present, Robert P. Howard, *Illinois: A History of the Prairie State* (Grand Rapids: William B. Eerdmans, 1972) can be recommended, though it is devoid of interpretation. Robert P. Sutton's two-volume reader, *The Prairie State* (Grand Rapids: William B. Eerdman's, 1976) is a thorough documentary history.

Pioneer life is brilliantly recaptured in loving detail in the Pulitzer Prize–winning, scholarly study by R. Carlyle Buley, *The Old Northwest: Pioneer Period, 1815–1840* (Bloomington, Ind.: Indiana University Press, 1950). Of the many excellent biographies of Lincoln, Albert J. Beveridge, *Abraham Lincoln, 1809–1858* (Boston: Houghton Mifflin Co., 1928) has the most complete information on Illinois life and politics. Paul Angle, *"Here I Have Lived": A History of Lincoln's Springfield, 1821–1865* (Chicago: Abraham Lincoln Books, 1971) is the best study of smalltown life, and Arthur C. Cole, *The Era of the Civil War, 1848–1870* (Springfield: Illinois Centennial Commission, 1919), one of six fine volumes of the Centennial History of Illinois, provides a full context for a critical era.

Developments in the late nineteenth and early twentieth century can be followed in Ernest L. Bogart and Charles Manfred Thompson, *The Industrial State, 1870–1893* (Springfield: Illinois Centennial Commission, 1920); in Forrest McDonald's insightful biography of *Insull*

(Chicago: University of Chicago Press, 1962); and in Richard J. Jensen, *The Winning of the Midwest: Social and Political Conflict, 1888–1896* (Chicago: University of Chicago Press, 1971), which deals with politics, religion, ethnic groups, and labor strife in Illinois and neighboring states. Lewis Atherton, *Main Street on the Middle Border* (Bloomington: Indiana University Press, 1954), thoroughly describes life in small towns at the turn of the century.

Recent history seldom attracts good scholarship, but a remarkable standout is Mary Watters, *Illinois in the Second World War*, 2 vols. (Springfield: Illinois Historical Library, 1951, 1952). Indeed, this is the best single study of Illinois, and the best history of any state from the late 1930s to the early postwar years. W. Lloyd Warner, *Democracy in Jonesville* (New York: Harper and Row, 1949) is a fair sociological study of Morris, in Grundy County, during the early 1940s. Medium-size cities are rarely treated with the sophistication that Daniel Elazar, *Cities of the Prairie* (New York: Basic Books, 1969) brings to his analysis of the political cultures of Springfield, Rockford, Decatur, Champaign-Urbana, Madison, and Saint Clair counties and the Quad Cities.

No city has been subjected to such close scholarly scrutiny as Chicago; unfortunately there is no modern one-volume history. However, Harold M. Mayer and Richard C. Wade, in *Chicago: Growth of a Metropolis* (Chicago: University of Chicago Press, 1969) have compiled a superbly illustrated book showing the historical development of all of Cook County. Among the specialized books on Chicago, the most informative are Hubert Nelli, *Italians of Chicago, 1880–1930* (New York: Oxford University Press, 1970); Perry Duis, *Chicago: Creating New Traditions* (Chicago: Chicago Historical Society, 1976) on 1890–1920; St. Clair Drake and Horace R. Cayton, *Black Metropolis: A Study of Negro Life in a Northern City* (New York: Harper and Row, 1945); and Carl Condit's impressive two volumes on architecture, city planning, and urban technology, *Chicago 1910–1929* and *Chicago, 1930–1970* (Chicago: University of Chicago Press, 1973, 1975).

Illinois politics is best approached through biographies, such as Robert Hartley, *Charles H. Percy: A Political Perspective* (Chicago: Rand-McNally & Co., 1975), Barbara Reynolds, *Jesse Jackson* (Chicago: Nelson-Hall, 1975), and John Barlow Martin, *Adlai Stevenson of Illinois* (Garden City, New York: Doubleday & Co., 1976). The latter is one of the most revealing books ever written about an American politician. Richard Daley has been the subject of numerous books. Mrs. Daley tried to suppress Mike Royko, *Boss* (New York: Dutton, 1971) from the racks of her local supermarket because it brilliantly embellishes every derogatory rumor abroad. More accurate, though less entertaining, is Bill Gleason, *Daley of Chicago* (New York: Simon and Schuster, 1970). Milton Rakove provides a balanced view in *Don't Make No Waves: An Insider's Analysis of the Daley Machine* (Bloomington: Indiana University Press, 1975). For a general picture of the state in the early 1970s, see the Illinois chapter in Neal R. Peirce, *The Megastates* (New York: W. W. Norton and Co., 1972). *Illinois Issues,* a monthly magazine published by Sangamon State University, is the best guide to current public affairs.

Index